DRUG ABUSE

Opposing Viewpoints®

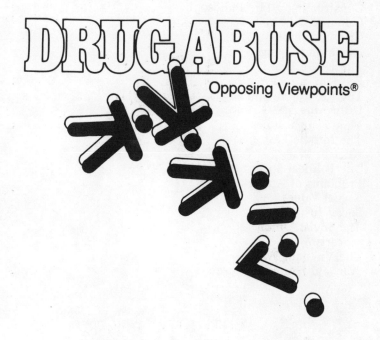

Other Books of Related Interest in the Opposing Viewpoints Series:

American Foreign Policy
Chemical Dependency
Mass Media

Additional Books in the Opposing Viewpoints Series:

Abortion
AIDS
American Government
American Values
America's Prisons
The Arms Race
Biomedical Ethics
Censorship
Central America
Constructing a Life Philosophy
Crime & Criminals
Criminal Justice
Death and Dying
The Death Penalty
Economics in America
The Environmental Crisis
Latin America
Male/Female Roles
The Middle East
Nuclear War
The Political Spectrum
Problems of Africa
Sexual Values
Social Justice
The Soviet Union
Terrorism
The Vietnam War
War and Human Nature

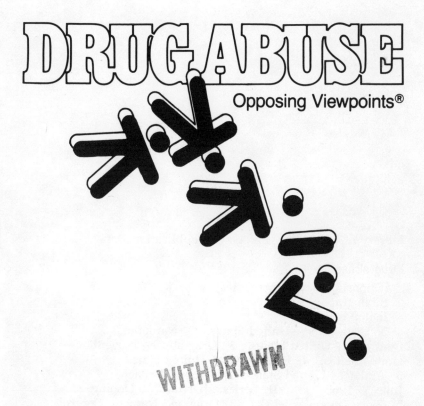

DRUG ABUSE

Opposing Viewpoints®

WITHDRAWN

David L. Bender & Bruno Leone, *Series Editors*

Julie S. Bach, *Book Editor*

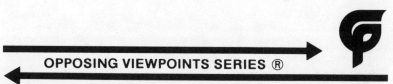

OPPOSING VIEWPOINTS SERIES ®

Greenhaven Press   577 Shoreview Park Road   St. Paul, Minnesota 55126

Library of Congress Cataloging-in-Publication Data

Drug abuse.

  (Opposing viewpoints series)
  Bibliography: p.
  Includes index.
  1. Drug abuse—United States. 2. Narcotics,
Control of—United States. 3. Drug abuse—Prevention—
United States. 4. Drug testing—United States.
5. Athletes—United States—Drug use. I. Bach,
Julie S., 1963-   . II. Series. [DNLM: 1. Doping
in Sports—popular works. 2. Drug and Narcotic Control
—popular works. 3. Street Drugs—popular works.
4. Substance Abuse—prevention & control—popular
works. WM 270 D7865]
HV5825.D7735 1988   362.2'93'0973   87-14837
ISBN 0-89908-426-5
ISBN 0-89908-401-X (pbk.)

"Congress shall make no law . . .
abridging the freedom of speech,
or of the press."

First Amendment to the US Constitution

The basic foundation of our democracy is the first amendment
guarantee of freedom of expression. The Opposing Viewpoints
books are dedicated to the concept of this basic freedom and the
idea that it is more important to practice it than to enshrine it.

Contents

Chapter 5: How Should Drugs Be Legally Prescribed?

Why Consider Opposing Viewpoints?

"It is better to debate a question without settling it than to settle a question without debating it."
Joseph Joubert (1754-1824)

The Importance of Examining Opposing Viewpoints

The purpose of the Opposing Viewpoints books, and this book in particular, is to present balanced, and often difficult to find, opposing points of view on complex and sensitive issues.

Probably the best way to become informed is to analyze the positions of those who are regarded as experts and well studied on issues. It is important to consider every variety of opinion in an attempt to determine the truth. Opinions from the mainstream of society should be examined. But also important are opinions that are considered radical, reactionary, or minority as well as those stigmatized by some other uncomplimentary label. An important lesson of history is the eventual acceptance of many unpopular and even despised opinions. The ideas of Socrates, Jesus, and Galileo are good examples of this.

Readers will approach this book with their own opinions on the issues debated within it. However, to have a good grasp of one's own viewpoint, it is necessary to understand the arguments of those with whom one disagrees. It can be said that those who do not completely understand their adversary's point of view do not fully understand their own.

A persuasive case for considering opposing viewpoints has been presented by John Stuart Mill in his work *On Liberty*. When examining controversial issues it may be helpful to reflect on this suggestion:

> The only way in which a human being can make some approach to knowing the whole of a subject, is by hearing what can be said about it by persons of every variety of opinion, and studying all modes in which it can be looked at by every character of mind. No wise man ever acquired his wisdom in any mode but this.

Analyzing Sources of Information

The Opposing Viewpoints books include diverse materials taken from magazines, journals, books, and newspapers, as well as statements and position papers from a wide range of individuals, organizations and governments. This broad spectrum of sources helps to develop patterns of thinking which are open to the consideration of a variety of opinions.

Pitfalls To Avoid

A pitfall to avoid in considering opposing points of view is that of regarding one's own opinion as being common sense and the most rational stance and the point of view of others as being only opinion and naturally wrong. It may be that another's opinion is correct and one's own is in error.

Another pitfall to avoid is that of closing one's mind to the opinions of those with whom one disagrees. The best way to approach a dialogue is to make one's primary purpose that of understanding the mind and arguments of the other person and not that of enlightening him or her with one's own solutions. More can be learned by listening than speaking.

It is my hope that after reading this book the reader will have a deeper understanding of the issues debated and will appreciate the complexity of even seemingly simple issues on which good and honest people disagree. This awareness is particularly important in a democratic society such as ours where people enter into public debate to determine the common good. Those with whom one disagrees should not necessarily be regarded as enemies, but perhaps simply as people who suggest different paths to a common goal.

Developing Basic Reading and Thinking Skills

In this book carefully edited opposing viewpoints are purposely placed back to back to create a running debate; each viewpoint is preceded by a short quotation that best expresses the author's main argument. This format instantly plunges the reader into the midst of a controversial issue and greatly aids that reader in mastering the basic skill of recognizing an author's point of view.

A number of basic skills for critical thinking are practiced in the activities that appear throughout the books in the series. Some of the skills are:

Evaluating Sources of Information The ability to choose from among alternative sources the most reliable and accurate source in relation to a given subject.

Separating Fact from Opinion The ability to make the basic distinction between factual statements (those that can be demonstrated or verified empirically) and statements of opinion (those that are beliefs or attitudes that cannot be proved).

Identifying Stereotypes The ability to identify oversimplified, exaggerated descriptions (favorable or unfavorable) about people and insulting statements about racial, religious or national groups, based upon misinformation or lack of information.

Recognizing Ethnocentrism The ability to recognize attitudes or opinions that express the view that one's own race, culture, or group is inherently superior, or those attitudes that judge another culture or group in terms of one's own.

It is important to consider opposing viewpoints and equally important to be able to critically analyze those viewpoints. The activities in this book are designed to help the reader master these thinking skills. Statements are taken from the book's viewpoints and the reader is asked to analyze them. This technique aids the reader in developing skills that not only can be applied to the viewpoints in this book, but also to situations where opinionated spokespersons comment on controversial issues. Although the activities are helpful to the solitary reader, they are most useful when the reader can benefit from the interaction of group discussion.

Using this book and others in the series should help readers develop basic reading and thinking skills. These skills should improve the readers' ability to understand what they read. Readers should be better able to separate fact from opinion, substance from rhetoric and become better consumers of information in our media-centered culture.

This volume of the Opposing Viewpoints books does not advocate a particular point of view. Quite the contrary! The very nature of the book leaves it to the reader to formulate the opinions he or she finds most suitable. My purpose as publisher is to see that this is made possible by offering a wide range of viewpoints which are fairly presented.

David L. Bender
Publisher

Introduction

"It is apparent to all but the most myopic that drug abuse affects the moral, social, and economic fabric of society."

Drug abuse is an increasingly serious problem for American society. In 1973 Dr. David Musto called it the "American disease." It is a disease for which no cure has been found.

According to the National Institute on Drug Abuse, substances such as cocaine, heroin, and PCP were implicated in 3,562 deaths in 1985. In that same year, over 100,000 hospital emergency room admissions involved illegal drugs. The Research Triangle Institute, a North Carolina think tank, estimates that Americans spend $110 billion a year to buy narcotics and lose perhaps $46.9 billion more in hidden costs to the economy. Some of these costs include decreased productivity, federally-paid hospital bills for drug addicts, and loss of tax revenue from undeclared income gained by selling illegal narcotics. President Reagan, in a televised speech, stated that drug abuse costs non-drug using Americans at least $60 billion a year.

The problem affects every segment of society from corporate executives to respected athletes to high school students and even small children. There is a vocal minority that believes drug abuse is not increasing and that drug use is not always harmful to society. However, as more frequent and dramatic drug-related problems touch the lives of individuals at all social and economic levels, the public has become alarmed. This has led to the development of a national War on Drugs, strongly supported by President and Mrs. Reagan. With the help of anti-drug organizations and media campaigns like "Just Say No," the Reagans and others have increased the focus on drug abuse.

Disagreement exists, however, on the best methods for eliminating this disease. For example, President Reagan has advocated drug testing for employees, a policy which members of the American Civil Liberties Union vehemently oppose. Members of the Drug Enforcement Administration have suggested using the US military to crack down on the drug trade, but foreign policy advisers have warned against such action. And while the International Olympic Committee has recommended mandatory drug testing for athletes, many coaches oppose such measures.

With such a wide variety of groups working to convince the public that their method of eliminating drugs is the right one or the most urgent, material on drug abuse is abundant. Organizations publish thousands of briefings, booklets, newsletters, warnings, and self-help guides. Editorials frequently address the problem of drug abuse. Books on drugs fill entire shelves in libraries. It is apparent to all but the most myopic that drug abuse affects the moral, social, and economic fabric of society.

Drug Abuse: Opposing Viewpoints explores some of the questions most often raised in the drug abuse controversy: How Should the War on Drugs Be Waged? Are International Drug Campaigns Effective? Should Drug Testing Be Used? What Should Be Done About the Drug Problem in Sports? and How Should Drugs Be Legally Prescribed? Like other anthologies in the Opposing Viewpoints series, it does not offer "right" answers. The editors have chosen these debates to provide an opportunity to examine the issue of drug abuse. They hope that the questions raised will provoke reflection on the implications of drug abuse for contemporary society.

CHAPTER 1

How Should the War on Drugs Be Waged?

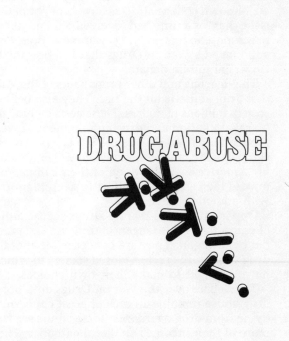

DRUG ABUSE

Chapter Preface

Drug abuse is a continuing problem in American society. Thousands of people undergo chemical dependency treatment every year, and millions more are believed to be addicted to narcotics. The easy accessibility of a new drug called "crack," a derivative of cocaine, and the tragic overdose deaths of several well-known college athletes have brought national attention to an issue that for a time had received only moderate publicity. Partly in response to this growing awareness, President and Mrs. Reagan announced a War on Drugs that has become the focus of a controversial public debate.

The Reagans and other proponents of the War on Drugs believe that drug abuse is on the rise. They also believe that it is costing society millions of dollars. These costs include the tax money spent on rehabilitation and drug enforcement as well as the impact on productivity of addicted workers. The proponents of the anti-drug campaign are most concerned, however, that drug abuse is harming America's youth. Much of their campaign has been directed toward teenagers in an effort to keep them from experimenting with addictive substances.

Opponents of this War on Drugs accuse anti-drug campaigners of exaggerating the dangers of drug use and jumping on a presidential bandwagon. They are concerned that zealous efforts to stop drug abuse will create a closed society in which people no longer have the right to make their own choices.

The debate over the War on Drugs does not cloud the fact that drug abuse remains an area of great concern. Teenagers are still dying from drug overdoses; some adults are still spending half or more of their incomes on illegal narcotics. The campaign against drugs will remain a national priority as long as the public feels threatened by the problem of drug abuse.

"Those who believe that people who use drugs aren't hurting anyone but themselves are wrong."

The War on Drugs Is Desperately Needed

Nancy Reagan

Nancy Reagan, First Lady of the United States, has spoken out strongly against drug abuse. She is largely responsible for the youth-oriented anti-drug campaign called "Just Say No." In the following viewpoint, excerpted from a speech delivered at the World Affairs Council, she explains her belief that drugs are harmful to society under any circumstance.

As you read, consider the following questions:

1. Why does the author believe drug abuse concerns everyone?
2. According to Reagan, what progress has been made in the war against drugs?
3. What further action does the author call for to stop drug abuse?

Nancy Reagan, in a speech delivered before the World Affairs Council in Los Angeles on June 24, 1986.

I want to talk about the battle against drugs.

Now before any of you can think to yourself, "Well, drug abuse really doesn't concern me," let me say it does concern you. It concerns you if you have a family, because drugs can unexpectedly tear a family to pieces—even the most loving families.

It concerns you as an employer, because drugs cost billions in illness, accidents, lost productivity and corruption.

It concerns you as a citizen, because there's a direct and undeniable link between crime and drugs. Law enforcement officers are being murdered in their efforts to protect our society from those who would destroy it with drugs.

And furthermore, it concerns you as an individual of conscience, because the tragedy and pain drugs cause are staggering.

An Epidemic

Ladies and gentlemen, there's a drug and alcohol epidemic in this country and no one is safe from its consequences—not you, not me, and certainly not our children. Drugs are a very powerful force in America, and we cannot ignore them.

Let me begin by taking you back, if I may, and telling you of my personal journey of awareness and commitment in regard to drug abuse . . . because in many ways my journey reflects that of the nation as a whole.

I first became aware of the problem in the 60s in Sacramento when my husband was Governor. To be honest, I really didn't understand the scope or the intensity of the problem then. Few of us did. But I knew something was happening to our children, something very tragic—even deadly.

I began getting calls from friends—calls of hurt and embarrassment and self-consciousness that their child could be on drugs—calls of confusion and ignorance about what was happening to their family, and on occasion calls of great pain at the loss of a son or daughter.

We were all so naive then.

Trying to raise children in the 60s was a terrifying experience. It seemed everything was against you—mainly your children. It was often hard—and still is—to tell the signs of drug abuse from normal adolescent rebellion. Parents didn't know where to turn, didn't know what to do.

In the movie, "The Dark at the Top of the Stairs," a woman says of her children, "I always wanted to give them life like a present, all wrapped up with every promise of happiness." This is what every parent wants for a child, but it was becoming painfully obvious, this wasn't the way it was to be.

As time went on, I got more calls. I began reading a little more about it in the papers. The age of the children involved seemed to be getting younger and younger. Clearly, we had the makings

Crashers

Clyde Peterson. Reprinted with permission.

of a tremendous problem.

Then when we moved to Washington I learned something. I learned that I had a chance to make a difference. I had a platform I would never have again and I should take advantage of it. Before I even got started though, March 30th and the attempted assassination happened—obviously my world stopped. But during the recuperation period, I met with doctors, teachers, and experts in the field of drug and alcohol abuse. For the first time, I began to understand the full frightening extent of the problem.

Yet all the statistics, all the clinical studies, all the expert briefings in the world can't match the reality of one deeply suffering young person. When people learned I was interested in drug abuse, I began getting letters that would simply pierce your heart, letters of pain and loneliness and confusion—thousands of them.

Joni

In the beginning, I got a letter from a 16-year-old girl I'll call Joni. I want to read it to you. Part of it's rather raw, but this letter tells you what drugs can do and tells it better than all the facts and figures I could present.

"Dear Mrs. Reagan, it has taken me many months to finally write you. At the age of 13 I was a regular user of anything and everything—pot, LSD, heroin, even nail polish remover, and if I was really desperate, liquid paper. I really don't know why I became a drug user, I guess because I never really liked myself, and now I hate myself even more.

"I destroyed my parents' hearts. Out of three boys, they thought their one and only little girl would follow their footsteps and be a good girl. I failed them . . . I hurt them. Because of what I've done, drugs have now affected my social and family life—I'm a loner, and it's all because of drugs.

"It got to the point where I was high all the time . . . for me, drugs were the escape from reality . . . to top it off, I was adopted as a baby, and when I found out I was different, I never wanted to be in the real world.

"Drugs are terrible, and it was a horrible, vicious cycle I lived in—drugs took me over. I can remember one time when I was high I needed a fix so bad, I had sex with a man around 55 years or older. For five hundred dollars worth of drugs, it was worth it at the time. I was once pregnant, but because of the drugs, I had the baby when it was five months into my pregnancy— the baby's arm was at its leg and its ear was at its cheek—the baby died.

"Drugs ruined my life, and I regret it so much. I long for the day when anyone will say to me, 'Joni, I love you—because of who you are, not who you were.' . . . Mrs. Reagan—please reach kids my age and younger—don't let what's happened to me and which destroyed my life happen to them."

Denying the Problem

How could anyone resist such a plea? But I realized our children's pleas weren't getting through to us. In fact, the whole problem of drug abuse was being denied. For too long our nation denied that a problem even existed. We denied that drug abuse had health and social consequences. We denied that anything could be done to counter widespread drug use.

There was almost a stigma in trying to take on drugs. It was unfashionable. It was illiberal and narrow-minded in our live-and-let-live society. Movies and television portrayed drugs as glamorous and cool. We heard a lot about the recreational use of drugs as if drugs were as harmless as Trivial Pursuit. Even law enforcement was weakened by the moral confusion surrounding drug abuse. It was as if all the people who sought to fight drugs had to justify their actions. As a matter of fact, no one was especially thrilled at the idea that this was what I wanted to do. And we had a lot of conversations about it.

Yet for five years now I've been trooping around this country and the world—over 100,000 miles, 53 cities in 28 states, 6 foreign countries, and countless interviews and television appearances. My main purpose when we started, was to raise the level of awareness in the country and to stress the importance of becoming knowledgeable about the danger of drug abuse.

A Resolute Stand

The victory of the drug culture is in no way assured if we maintain a resolute stand against it. We know that we can do better on all aspects of drug policy. We can make effective international action against the drug traffic a high priority of our foreign policy, and thus score decisively in the effort to stop the smugglers before they reach our shores. We can give our Federal enforcement agencies the means they need to do their work with maximum effectiveness. The Federal government can provide better assistance to state and local agencies. Washington can assume a larger, more appropriate role in the eradication of domestic marijuana cultivation. These are all enforcement gains that are just waiting to be made.

Charles B. Rangel, *USA Today*, May 1984.

I think we've succeeded in that. I certainly see more about drug abuse in the papers and on television. More well-known people are coming forward and talking about their addiction. Slowly, the wall of denial seems to be crumbling.

We now have 9,000 parent groups, which sprang up independently and are doing marvelous work in closing down head-shops, becoming involved in school drug programs, and forming support groups for one another.

Just Say No

I always thought if we could just get the young people involved it would be a giant step forward. And now that's happening with the "Just Say No" clubs. Young people are forming their own positive peer groups to counter the pressures to use drugs. It's sometimes hard to believe how complex our children's lives are today—in my day peer pressure meant your saddle shoes had to be dirty.

21

Internationally, we're also making progress. I've twice invited the First Ladies of other countries here to discuss the drug abuse problem and to let them hear from experts and young people who are former addicts. The numbers of these concerned First Ladies is rapidly growing and their influence is being felt around the world. The first time we had 17 acceptances, the second time we had 30 acceptances. I was very gratified to learn that as a result of those meetings there are now parents groups in Germany, Portugal, Malaysia, Ireland, and Thailand. Hopefully, these will grow even more.

I feel very good that we've succeeded in raising the level of awareness. We are more aware of drug abuse than ever before— but now it's time for the next step.

It's time to let people know they have a moral responsibility to do more than simply recognize the problem. They have an obligation to take a personal stand against drugs.

You know, one young girl wrote to me about her brother, who had helped raise her. She still loved him despite the fact he'd become so possessed by drugs he's even threatened to kill them both. She wrote, "One day he was so drugged up that he couldn't walk, he sat on a step and gave me a look of 'help me' straight in the eyes. I started to cry. Later that night we found out he overdosed on heroin. . . . He hurt me so bad, but never bad enough that I hated him. I love him more than anyone knows. . . . " At the bottom of her letter in large plaintive letters she wrote, "Help!"

A Moral Obligation

Ladies and gentlemen, each of you has a moral obligation to provide that help. I don't mean you have to work in a drug rehabilitation center or join a parents group. But you do have the responsibility to put your conscience and principles on the line. You have the responsibility to be intolerant of drug use anywhere, anytime, by anybody. You have the responsibility of forcing the issue to the point of making others uncomfortable and yourself unpopular.

Those who believe that people who use drugs aren't hurting anyone but themselves are wrong. Drugs hurt society. The money spent on drugs goes into the hands of one of the most ruthless, despicable lots ever to breathe—the drug producers. They are often murderers. They are sometimes terrorists. They are always criminals. They represent man at his most debased. They are the people who are financing the death and destruction of our young people.

And by doing nothing when you know of drug use, you're conspiring with them as they line their pockets with even more blood money.

I have a message for the drug dealers and producers and pushers, and the message is this: The parents throughout the world are going to drive you out of business. We're the ones who are going to be the pushers from now on. We're going to push *you* out. Push you out of our schools, out of our neighborhoods, out of our communities, and out of existence!

There's nothing remarkable about how we'll do it. We'll do it through education and commitment. We'll do it through individual responsibility. We're going to dry up the dealers' markets. We're going to make the poison they push as worthless as they are. We're going to take the customer away from the product.

Never Give In

Can you imagine being young and yet without the spark and enthusiasm of youth? Can you imagine being young and yet an empty shell of vacant stares, vacant emotions, and vacant hopes? Can you imagine not caring about anything in this entire world except the chemical you're going to force into your body? That is what it means to be young and possessed by drugs.

Joining the War Against Drugs

I'd like you to remember that controlling the drug problem is a responsibility shared by us all. . . .

We all have a job to do as parents, as community leaders, and as good citizens. It's not the other guy's job—it's yours. You have to do your part to put zero tolerance for drug abuse on top of the agenda wherever you are, at work or at home. It is going to take that kind of support . . . to turn the drug problem around. It's going to be your example that is going to make the difference.

William F. Alden, in a speech to the American Society of Industrial Security, Orlando, Florida, June 24, 1986.

You have a moral duty to prevent this loss. You have the responsibility to be intolerant of drugs and to be forceful in your intolerance. You have the obligation to remember the words of Whittier, who unwittingly explained the essential tragedy of drug abuse among our young:

"For of all the sad words of tongue or pen, the saddest are these:
It might have been."

I've often been asked, well, don't you get discouraged? Doesn't it seem like the problem is so big that it can't possibly be overcome? And I refuse to say yes to that. I don't believe that's true. I believe when you say that, it becomes a self-fulfilling prophesy, for one thing. And every time I'm reminded of those wonderful words of Winston Churchill's when he said, "never give in, never give up, never, never, never."

"The attempt to suppress the use of drugs is as futile as the wish to teach cooking to an ape."

The War on Drugs Is Hypocritical

Lewis H. Lapham

Lewis H. Lapham is the editor of *Harper's Magazine*, a monthly literary magazine. In the following viewpoint, he contends that the government's war on drugs is only a hypocritical attempt to ignore deeper societal problems. Something should be done about drug abuse, Lapham concedes, but current federal efforts have been insincere and have contributed to the illusive belief that America can do no wrong. Until the country is willing to recognize its shortcomings, says Lapham, no attempt to curb drug abuse will be successful.

As you read, consider the following questions:

1. How does Lapham describe America's view of itself?
2. What examples does the author use to show that the government does not sincerely intend to eliminate drug-related crime?
3. What point does the author make by comparing the war on drugs to the war in Vietnam?

The world can ill spare any vice which has obtained long and large among civilized people. Such a vice must have some good along with its deformities.
Samuel Butler

As every schoolchild learns before he or she reaches the age of ten, America is always and forever innocent. Foreigners commit crimes against humanity. Americans make well-intentioned mistakes. Foreigners incite wars, embrace communism, sponsor terrorists, and smuggle cocaine into Connecticut. Americans cleanse the world of its impurities.

True, a few hundred thousand peasants might come to grief in Southeast Asia because of an American mistake. True, American corporations enhance the yields of their industry with their talent for price-fixing, theft, loan-sharking, and fraud. But their crimes, being American, can be understood as temporary breakdowns in the otherwise flawless machinery of the American soul. The fault is never one of character or motive. Americans receive their virtue from heaven, as part of their inheritance and a proof of their natural aptitude for goodness.

Maintaining an Illusion

The illusion of grace is even more expensive to maintain than the nation's $60-billion-a-year drug habit. Devoted to the ceaseless rituals of purification, the nation spends as much on soap and cosmetics as it does on nuclear weapons, the object of both expenditures being the protection of the American self against contamination by foreign substances.

Even the meanest of American politicians has no choice but to become a social hygenist. President and Mrs. Reagan, of course, set the standard of virtuoso performance, and on September 14 [1986] they appeared in concert on television to announce "a national crusade" against the use of drugs. The President said, "Let us not forget who we are. Drug abuse is a repudiation of everything America is." Mrs. Reagan, with whom the President was holding hands, said, "There is no moral middle ground."

If their concern hadn't been so unctuous, and their voices not quite so sweet, their announcement might have seemed less like the scattering of incense and the tinkling of tiny bells.

Cowardice and Incompetence

The worry about drugs provides a ceremonial entertainment for politicians anxious to distract attention from their habitual cowardice and incompetence. . . . Congress hurriedly took up a bill meant to add another $1.5 billion to the $2 billion already assigned to the labor of purification. In New York Mayor Koch asked for troops to defend the city's perimeters. Elsewhere in the country the voices of civic sanitation, heeding Mrs. Reagan's call to "create

25

an outspoken intolerance for drug use," recommended shooting suspected drug dealers on sight. An eleven-year-old girl in Los Angeles reported her parents to the police when she found a marijuana plant in her own garden. A prominent editor in the headquarters tent of the *New York Times* was heard to remark that it might not be a bad idea if somebody's Christian air force bombed the coca plantations in Colombia.

Ben Sargent. Reprinted with permission.

In the midst of the singing of psalms, nobody had the bad manners to ask why it is that Americans have become so fond of drugs. Nor did anybody embarrass the choir by pointing out that (a) the attempt to suppress the use of drugs is as futile as the wish to teach cooking to an ape, and that (b) the government—whether municipal, state, or federal—has little intention of reducing the crime implicit in the drug traffic.

Simple Arithmetic

The simplest arithmetic demonstrates the lack of honest intent. New York City currently assigns eight judges to hear 20,000 narcotics cases a year (which means roughly 19,200 cases become matters for plea bargain), and the average length of time spent in jail as a result of a drug arrest amounts to seven days. The city obviously hasn't got the money to hire enough judges, deploy enough police spies, build enough jails. The same arithmetic pertains everywhere else in the country. If Congress or the Reagans mean what they say, they would be obliged to amass a defense fund on the order of $50 to $70 billion a year, almost all of it directed toward education. But they don't mean what they say, and almost everybody familiar with the catalogue of human desire knows they don't mean what they say. Every district attorney understands that the laws cannot be enforced; so does every judge, detective, addict, literary agent, and brothel-keeper. Marijuana is now one of America's principal cash crops, comparable to corn or wheat or soybeans. (Pursued to its logical end, the *Realpolitik* suggested by the gentleman at the *New York Times* would entail the bombing of California.) The number of people addicted to drugs of all descriptions possibly reflects the prevalence of fear and unhappiness at all ranks of American society, but the statistics testify just as eloquently to the common pleasures of the senses. The making of vindictive laws merely inflates the price of drugs and increases the profit margins in the smuggling trades.

The faith in the miracle of aimless force bears comparison to the American policy in Vietnam. The commanders of our air force knew as early as 1966 that their program of heavy bombing had failed to transform the North Vietnamese into submissive and enthusiastic subscribers to *Time*. Rather than admit their failure, the commanders ordered more and heavier bombing. Similarly, the managers of the President's crusade against drugs, well aware that they'll never reach Jerusalem, doggedly order more laws, more urine tests, more arrests. . . .

Lack of Serious Desire

If either the government or the society were serious in the desire to reduce the crime and human suffering supported by the drug trades, Congress could transform narcotics into substances as legal as alcohol, pornography, or tobacco. Deprived of its romance as well as of its profit, the drug business might follow the automobile business into bankruptcy.

But the Reagan Administration, like the vast majority of the American people, prefers the purity of its illusions. The society chooses to believe that the world's evil doesn't reside in men but exists, like the air, in the space between them. The Pentagon has so refined the use of euphemism that it now defines war as "violence processing." After the American defeat in Vietnam, Arthur M. Schlesinger, obligingly washing the sheets of the American conscience, pronounced the war "a tragedy without villians."

To the extent that drug addiction can be defined as a foreign conspiracy—a consequence not of the ancient human predicament but of new export strategies in Bolivia—Americans can take com-

27

fort in their righteousness. Like the late Howard Hughes hiding under gauze on the roof of a Las Vegas hotel from the armies of invading bacteria (a.k.a. Bolivians, communists, cigarette smoke, the AIDS virus, etc.), the innocent nation invariably discovers itself betrayed—by events, by its doctors or servants, by radioactive clouds or a collision of oil tankers off the coast of Peru, by terrorists and travel agents and the unseen trolls manipulating the levers of history.

The Drug Frenzy

America finds itself in the grip of a frenzy over the "drug crisis." How can this be, with all that has been done? Some blame the "pushers." Others rightly point out that there is demand as well as supply, and also blame the users. In fact, there is good reason to believe that the government itself, for all that it has proclaimed yet another war on drugs, has been one of the most potent causes of the current crisis. . . .

Government policy has aggravated our society's chronic problems with drugs by mounting a propaganda and enforcement campaign that erodes crucial distinctions between more and less dangerous drugs, makes the marketing of the more dangerous variety the preferred option for dealers, and increases health risks, crime, and corruption.

Richard C. Cowan, *National Review*, December 5, 1986.

Together with his most ardent admirers, President Reagan has no wish to see, much less govern, an America that doesn't conform to the pictures on the postcards. The failure of his imagination corresponds to the public wish to know as little as possible about the infinite variety of human expression and desire. Nor does the public wish to be reminded of an America in which illiterate children commit murder for the price of a secondhand radio; in which, contrary to the publicity appearing in *Fortune* and *Vanity Fair*, most business ventures end in debt or failure; in which hospitals resemble prisons and the prisons have become as crowded as resort hotels—a nation inhabited not by the smiling faces seen on the postcards but by people so frightened or intimidated that they have no choice but to sell, in a falling market, what little remains to them of their self-respect, and who, to their sorrow, all too easily find a buyer in a police official, a corporation, or a pimp. It is their grief and dejection of spirit that changes them into statistics or commodities, not their country of origin, the books they read, or their failure to take regular baths.

"The adult legalization of those illicit drugs we are unable to control effectively would be a wiser policy."

Legalize Illegal Drugs

Ernest van den Haag and John E. LeMoult

Ernest van den Haag is John M. Olin professor of jurisprudence and public policy at Fordham University in New York City. John E. LeMoult writes frequently on legal issues. In Part I of the following viewpoint, van den Haag compares current drug laws to alcohol prohibition of the 1920s. He believes that arguments for prohibiting drugs are no more persuasive than were arguments for prohibiting alcohol. LeMoult, in Part II, agrees, adding that legalizing drugs could reduce crime considerably.

As you read, consider the following questions:

1. Why does van den Haag use the example of alcohol prohibition?
2. According to van den Haag, what are three major drawbacks to the current prohibition of drugs?
3. Why, according to LeMoult, would crime be dealt a shattering blow if drugs were legalized?

Ernest van den Haag, "Legalize Those Drugs We Can't Control," *The Wall Street Journal*, August 8, 1985. Reprinted with the author's permission.
John E. LeMoult, "Legalize Drugs," *The New York Times*, June 15, 1984. Copyright © 1984 by The New York Times Company. Reprinted by permission.

I

More than 2,200 federal, state and local law-enforcement officers launched a massive series of raids in an effort to eradicate domestically cultivated marijuana. Attorney General Edwin Meese flew to the scene of raids in Arkansas to dramatize the Reagan administration's commitment to the project. But notwithstanding this display of resolve, U.S. drug-enforcement policies are likely to be a continuing failure. Although I am a strong political conservative, I now believe that the costs of our fruitless struggle against illegal drugs are not worth the modest benefits likely to be achieved. However distasteful the prospect, the adult legalization of those illicit drugs we are unable to control effectively would be a wiser policy.

Prohibition

A glance back into American history is instructive. Because of the notoriously harmful effects that alcohol can have, its sale was prohibited in 1919. A large industry soon grew up to provide it. Drinks remained easily available. Since the industry providing them was illegal, it required organizations outside the law to enforce contracts and collect debts. This led to the growth of major criminal entities that used the unlawful money earned to bribe and corrupt law-enforcement agencies. Prohibition ended by significantly debasing the political life of the nation, and there is no evidence it reduced alcoholism.

When the public finally realized that prohibition could not be enforced, the law was repealed in 1933. From this one may infer a general principle. In a democracy one can regulate, but one cannot effectively prohibit, sumptuary activities desired by a substantial segment of the population. Unenforceable attempts to prohibit certain substances will cause more harm than good.

Prohibition could not delegitimize a long tradition of social drinking, and moderate drinkers felt that they should not be deprived because others drank more than they should. However, drug taking is hardly ever justified as a legitimate or moderate social pleasure. People feel that drugs always lead to addiction, so there is far more support for prohibiting drugs than there was for prohibiting alcohol.

But does the prohibition of addictive drugs prevent enough harm to justify the cost? We have too many alcoholics, but there is no evidence that the rate of alcoholism has risen because of the repeal of Prohibition. Granted, then, that drugs have harmful effects, would legalization lead to worse effects than the legalization of alcohol? Perhaps, but it does not seem so.

Taking drugs does not necessarily addict you. In practice, drugs were cheap and freely available to U.S. soldiers in Vietnam. Except for those engaged in combat, a small minority at any time,

30

our soldiers were thoroughly bored. They found themselves in a foreign land, with little to do, without family and friends, and in the midst of a population whose language and customs they did not understand. Most of them used alcohol as well as some drugs. Some used drugs regularly. But only a few became addicted to them. And most of these addicts stopped with little difficulty after returning to the U.S.

Drugs also are easily available in many of the countries from which we import them. Yet the populations of these countries have not become addicted because addiction is self-limiting. If the substances are readily available, a certain proportion of the population becomes addicted; most people do not.

Change the Law

The profits from illegal drug trafficking generate billions of dollars, billions that submerge and then absorb banks, billions that buy judges, businesses, real estate and the ears of the politically powerful—if not their souls.

That puts these drugs in a special category, but it is a category made special by the law itself. Change the law, and you narrow the problem to its health component. Repeal today's version of prohibition, in other words, and you are free to spend the sums now going into failed law enforcement on the vastly more important areas of scientific research and public education.

Hodding Carter III, *The Wall Street Journal*, August 14, 1986.

There are several ways of legalizing drugs. In Britain drugs are legally available from designated clinics for certified addicts. We have done something of the sort with methadone. It has not worked all that well. If prescription drugs are necessary for heroin or cocaine an illegal market is likely, and it exists in Britain. To avoid it drugs must be made as legal as alcohol is. Legalization only for certified addicts would not solve the problem.

Drawbacks to Prohibition

Drugs now are quite readily available. Still, once legalized, they would become cheaper and more accessible to people who previously had not tried them, because of the high price or the legal risk. Does the likely rise of addiction warrant the continuation of prohibition? Or would it be minor? Any projection is highly speculative—just as any projection of a rise of alcoholism after repeal would have been. Yet a significant rise in drug addiction seems unlikely. After all, heroin users, though often poor, manage to come up with the price (often by committing crimes). And the user, as distinguished from the dealer, currently runs a very low legal risk.

The current prohibition of the importation and sale of drugs has three major drawbacks.

- Attempts to enforce prohibitions are very costly (federal law enforcement alone cost $1.22 billion in fiscal 1985) and constantly increasing.

- Prohibitions are ineffective. It is generally estimated that no more than 10% of all the drugs imported are actually confiscated. Increased efforts are likely to be only marginally effective. Thus, our present policy mainly raises the price of drugs. This might as well be done by appropriate taxation. Some of the revenue could then be used for anti-drug education.

- The outlawing of drugs has produced major criminal activity, beyond the sale and importation of drugs themselves, involving frequent murders and major corruption. Even draconian penalties will not avail; people are willing to risk death for the immense profits that can be made owing to the prohibition.

Legalization of marijuana, cocaine and heroin—the major drugs against which the government is now engaged in a Sisyphean struggle—does not imply that other drugs have to be legalized. Libertarian ideologues argue for making all drugs of all kinds freely available without requiring prescriptions. This is not my argument. I would continue to require prescriptions for drugs such as barbiturates that have a potential for abuse or are dangerous in inexpert hands—as long as they can be controlled effectively. My argument for the legalization of marijuana, cocaine and heroin rests on the fact that their prohibition can no more be effective than the prohibition of alcohol.

II

As a trial lawyer with some 20 years' experience, I have followed the battle against drugs with a keen interest. Month after month, we have read stories of how the Government has made a major seizure of drugs and cracked an important drug ring. It is reassuring to know that for more than 20 years our Federal, state and local governments have been making such headway against drugs. It reminds me of the body counts during the Vietnam War, when every week we heard of large numbers of North Vietnamese and Vietcong soldiers killed in battle. Somehow, they kept coming, and they finally forced us out and overwhelmed their enemies.

Every elected official from President Reagan on down goes through the ritual of calling for stiffer enforcement of drug and trafficking laws. The laws get stricter, and more and more billions of dollars are spent on the police, courts, judges, jails, customs inspectors and informants. But the drugs keep coming, keep growing, leaking into this country through thousands of little holes.

Traffic is funded by huge financial combines and small entrepreneurs. Drugs are carried by organized-crime figures and ordinary people. The truth is, the stricter the enforcement, the more money there is in smuggling.

Legalization is not a new idea. But perhaps it is time to recognize that vigorous drug enforcement will not plug the holes. Perhaps it is time to think the unthinkable. What would happen if we legalized heroin, cocaine, marijuana and other drugs? What if they were regulated like liquor and with the protections provided for over-the-counter drugs? Would we turn into a nation of spaced-out drug addicts?

Part of Society

Drugs have been a part of our society for some time. The first anti-drug laws in the United States were passed in 1914. They were really anti-Chinese laws, because people on the West Coast were alarmed at the rise of opium dens among Chinese immigrants. Before that, there were plenty of opium addicts in the United States, but they were mostly white middle-class women who took laudanum (then available over the counter) because it was considered unacceptable for women to drink alcohol.

Reaching for Their Rights

History shows us that when millions of Americans want something, they'll do anything to get it—even to the point of deciding that the law is wrong and that it needs changing. In fact, until a series of laws were passed in 1914-1936, Americans had uncontrolled access to what we now call "controlled" substances.

Whenever Americans have heard that their government "knows best," they have reached for their rights—and that's what millions of our citizens are telling authorities by their daily decisions.

John Howell, *Harper's Magazine*, March 1986.

After the first laws were passed, and more drugs added to the forbidden list, the sale of heroin and other drugs shifted to the ghettos, where men desperate for money were willing to risk prison to make a sale. Middle-class addicts switched to alcohol. Today, one in 10 Americans is an alcohol addict. It is accepted. The number of addicts of heroin and other drugs is tiny compared with the number of alcoholics. But these drugs cause 10 times the amount of crime caused by alcohol.

What would happen if the other drugs were legal? Many experts believe there would be no increase in the number of drug addicts. They speak of an addictive personality and say that if such a person cannot easily obtain one drug he will become addicted to another. Many feel that the legalization of heroin and other drugs would mean that such addictive types would change from alcohol to other drugs. A 1972 Ford Foundation study showed that addiction to these other drugs is no more harmful than addiction to alcohol.

A Blow to Crime

But what about crime? Overnight it would be dealt a shattering blow. Legal heroin and cocaine sold in drugstores, only to people over 21, and protected by our pure food and drug laws, would sell at a very small fraction of its current street value. The adulterated and dangerous heroin concoctions available today for $20 from your friendly pusher would, in clean form with proper dosage on the package, sell for about 50 cents in a drugstore. There would be no need for crime.

With addicts no longer desperate for money to buy drugs, mugging and robbery in our major cities would be more than cut in half. The streets would be safer. There would be no more importers, sellers and buyers on the black market. It would become uneconomical. Huge crime rings would go out of business.

More than half the crime in America is drug related. But drugs themselves do not cause crime. Crime is caused by the law against drugs and the need of addicts to steal money for their purchase. Overnight the cost of law enforcement, courts, judges, jails and convict rehabilitation would be cut in half. The savings in taxes would be more than $50 billion a year.

We may not be ready for a radical step of this kind. Perhaps we are willing to spend $50 billion a year and suffer the unsafe streets to express our moral opposition to drugs. But we should at least examine the benefits of legalization. We should try to find out whether drug use would dramatically increase, what the tax savings would be. I do not suggest that we legalize drugs immediately. I ask only that we give it some thought.

"It is time to escalate the war on drugs, not to capitulate by legalizing these substances."

Do Not Legalize Illegal Drugs

Charles B. Rangel

Charles B. Rangel is chairman of the US House of Representatives Select Committee on Narcotics Abuse and Control. In the following viewpoint, he argues that a public policy to reduce both the supply of and demand for drugs would be far more effective than legalizing them. Representative Rangel believes that legalization would be giving in to drug dealers and would only increase the nation's drug abuse problem.

As you read, consider the following questions:

1. According to Rangel, why does the present failure to control drug abuse not justify legalization?
2. What are "non-deterrables"? How are they used in the argument to legalize drugs? How does the author refute this argument?

Charles B. Rangel, letter to the editor of *Harper's Magazine*, March 1986. Reprinted with the author's permission.

As chairman of the U.S. House of Representatives' Select Committee on Narcotics Abuse and Control, I read with interest the forum "What Is Our Drug Problem?" [*Harper's Magazine*, December 1985]. While I concur with many of the observations made by the participants, I find some of the rhetoric and alternatives to be defeatist.

It is true that the trafficking in and abuse of narcotic and psychotropic substances have increased. Despite record seizures of illegal substances by enforcement agencies, record quantities remain a threat to our citizens. Yet the short-term inability to control the problem does not justify proposals to abandon current policies. Although our drug problem has grown, this has been in the face of our best law enforcement efforts rather than because of them.

In short, our current policies have had a marginal deterrent effect. There is no telling how big the addict population and the supply of drugs would be if drugs were to become legal. Arguing, in a different context, for capital punishment, Ernest van den Haag has asserted that the burden of proof lies with death penalty opponents to demonstrate that capital punishment produces no marginal return. Applying his argument to narcotics control, the burden of proof rests with those . . . who seek to legalize these substances. They have not proven their position.

Reducing Supply and Demand

That is not to say our current policies are wholly adequate. What is needed is a public policy that will result in a reduced supply of drugs as well as a reduced demand for them. This means federal, state, and local education, treatment, and prevention programs, that are well designed and adequately funded; cooperative and appropriately funded law enforcement efforts; and effective use of diplomacy and foreign aid to support countries attempting to control narcotics production and trafficking and to induce those that are not to do so. If both supply and demand are reduced in a balanced fashion, there will be less likelihood of increased consumption and/or increased availability.

A demand-reduction strategy encompasses treatment, prevention, and education. I find it noteworthy that the forum participants agreed that there is a need for education, although they disagreed as to what the content of that education should be. I strongly disagree . . . that we must begin teaching people the responsible use of mind-altering substances. The more we learn about the long-term effects of using drugs, even marijuana, the more we come to understand that no drug can be labeled harmless. The aim of federal policy is not to frighten adolescents, . . . but to provide informed and up-to-date medical evidence, which supports the conclusion that the only sane and responsible approach to social and recreational drug usage is to say no.

That law enforcement is part of the supply-reduction strategy is evident, but it is also part of the demand-reduction strategy. In drawing the line between what is and is not permissible, criminal law is directed toward not only the lawbreakers but the law-abiding. The message communicated by the law in this century is that recreational drug use is not acceptable behavior. This message is consistent with our traditions. Legalizing substances such as cocaine, marijuana, and heroin would send a message to our young people that drug use is socially acceptable and will not harm them. This message is not only inconsistent with our traditions but also untrue. Thus, the "moral educative" function of criminal law dictates the continued proscription of drugs.

"Non-Deterrables"

Moreover, I believe it is naive to think that if there were a relaxation of legal restraints on drugs, the criminal would go away or be satisfied with non-threatening pursuits. Even van den Haag, in his work on the death penalty, acknowledges that there are always non-deterrables. Should we change our laws to allow certain behavior because some people are not deterred? I think not.

Reduction of demand is necessary but not sufficient; there must also be a reduction in the supply of narcotics. Supply is most

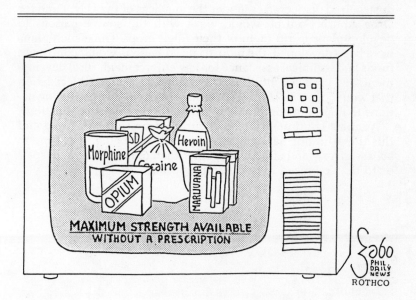

© Szabo/Rothco

vulnerable to eradication where it originates as an agricultural crop. While the Reagan Administration has claimed to be waging a war against drugs, it is, in fact, the Congress that has voted to cut off all aid, other than anti-narcotics and humanitarian aid, to countries such as Peru and Bolivia—countries that have ignored their obligation to the Single Convention on Narcotic Drugs, which requires that they wipe out illicit crop cultivation.

On a . . . seventeen-day trip to Latin America, the Select Committee met with top officials of seven nations—Colombia, Ecuador, Peru, Bolivia, Brazil, Argentina, and Uruguay. The leaders of these countries told us that if we do not move quickly to help them, their countries will fall into the hands of the drug traffickers or fall prey to anti-democratic forces, which can appear to be a stable alternative in the chaos created by the traffickers. We need to use diplomacy more effectively and to allocate adequate resources to help the producer countries eliminate illicit cultivation.

Escalate the War

It is time to escalate the war on drugs, not to capitulate by legalizing these substances. To support this effort, I have proposed three initiatives. First, I have introduced the State and Local Assistance Act of 1985. It provides for grants to state and local governments to assist them in drug law enforcement and drug abuse treatment. Second, I have proposed a new U.N. initiative whereby the industrialized democracies, under the auspices of the U.N. Fund for Drug Abuse Control, would work with the source nations to develop plans to rid them of their illicit crops. Once such plans have been developed, the industrialized nations would contribute funds and technical assistance for law enforcement, rural development, and crop substitution. Third, I have introduced legislation that would deny most-favored-nation status to drug-producing nations that are not complying with their drug control obligations.

We must continue to fight to curtail drug trafficking and end this threat to our national security and well-being. It is time to act assertively and effectively, rather than to fall victim to despair or to be victimized by utopian proposals. ·

"It's time to commit our armed forces to help in the battle against drug smugglers."

Use Military Intervention in the War on Drugs

Edward I. Koch and Edwin Meese III

Edward I. Koch is the mayor of New York City. Edwin Meese III is attorney general of the United States and chairman of the interagency National Drug Enforcement Policy Board. In Part I of the following viewpoint, Koch explains that government agencies presently responsible for stopping the drug trade have too few resources. They could benefit greatly from military assistance. In Part II, Meese argues that the drug epidemic in America is serious enough to warrant using the armed forces.

As you read, consider the following questions:

1. Why, according to Koch, have government agencies been unable to stop drug trafficking across US borders?
2. Why does Koch believe the armed forces would be successful in the war on drugs?
3. According to Meese, why does the drug problem warrant intervention by the military?

Edwin Meese III, "Another Option in the Fight Against Drugs," *The Washington Post National Weekly Edition*, August 8, 1986. © The Washington Post.
Edward I. Koch, "Turn Armed Forces Loose in War on Drugs," *Minneapolis Star and Tribune*, July 8, 1985. © Edward I. Koch.

I

The massive illicit drug traffic can be stopped only by the direct involvement of our armed forces. This is what Congress must authorize.

The General Accounting Office ... reported [in 1985] that federal agencies seize only 16 percent of the marijuana and less than 10 percent of the heroin and cocaine that comes into the country each year. The Customs Service says it intercepts only one out of every 100 planes flying cocaine and heroin into the country.

There were 18,000 such flights in 1983.

But Customs Commissioner William Von Raab offers little hope. He says he doesn't "like statistics. I don't know what is served by using them." Small surprise. "For those who thought customs was in any way guarding our borders," he reported after two years as commissioner, "we weren't."

How can it? The head of the Drug Enforcement Administration (DEA) said ... that to curtail the flow of drugs effectively he'd need 40,000 agents. He has only 1,900 worldwide.

Inadequate Resources

The Coast Guard has no more than 10 boats patrolling the entire southeastern coast and Gulf of Mexico, the principal channel through which the bulk of illegal cocaine and marijuana enters our territory. In 1984 the Coast Guard intercepted only two boats in the waters off New York.

There are no radar installations designed to detect drug flights over our southern coast. The DEA has only eight planes with sufficient overtake speed to police the border from Key West to San Diego.

Our Border Patrol has no look-down, low-altitude radar, only a few interceptor jets with tracking radar, and only a small force of the large, fast helicopters needed to transport agents to landing sites when suspect aircraft are forced to land.

The illegal narcotics trade is a $110 billion annual business, but the entire federal drug-abuse budget totals only $1.5 billion. Only about two-thirds of this figure is committed to law-enforcement programs, including prosecution, prisons and Internal Revenue Service auditors.

You can't win a war without weapons. Until the weapons are committed, the drug invaders will have a virtual free pass across our borders.

Help in the Battle

That's why it's time to commit our armed forces to help in the battle against drug smugglers. The federal Posse Comitatus Act places significant constraints on military involvement in drug interdiction. Clearly prohibited are "interdiction of a vehicle, vessel, aircraft or other similar activity, and the use of military personnel for surveillance or pursuit of individuals."

The danger in such constraints was apparent on July 17, 1983.

On that day the Kidd, a naval vessel with a six-man Coast Guard unit aboard, was on patrol in our southern territorial waters when it encountered a suspect ship flying a foreign flag. The ship was stopped, but refused boarding.

The Kidd learned the ship was not registered in the country it claimed and, therefore, was a stateless ship that could be legally boarded, but only by the Coast Guard. Fearing its intervention would violate the Posse Comitatus Act, the Navy sought instruction from the Defense Department as it trailed the vessel.

Eventually, a Coast Guard flag was raised and the Kidd became a Coast Guard vessel. When its crew was finally allowed to board the pirate ship, a cache of drugs was seized. Though necessary, this stretching of the law illustrates the urgent need to revise the Posse Comitatus Act.

Direct Involvement

Rep. Charles Bennett, D.-Fla., has introduced an amendment authorizing the direct involvement of the armed forces in the interdiction of illegal drug smuggling outside the land areas of the United States when requested by the head of a federal drug-enforcement agency.

The Military Could Do More

When Congress enabled the military to become involved in the fight against drugs, many of us hoped that military equipment, personnel and technology would be put into the field—as finally they have been in Bolivia. But Bolivia is only one front in this war. Many countries use their military in the fight against drugs, and since the Defense Department's budget is $315 billion a year—almost $1 billion a day—the Navy and the Air Force could certainly do more in the real war being waged on our borders and coastlines where there are live bullets—and people dying.

Peter B. Bensinger, *Newsweek*, July 28, 1986.

The Bennett amendment, cosponsored by Rep. Charles Rangel, D.-N.Y., the chairman of the House Select Committee on Narcotics Abuse and Control, will resolve the legal ambiguities that led to the Kidd incident.

It has been suggested that the assignment of the military to the role of interdicting drug trafficking would divert crucial personnel and resources from the primary mission of the armed forces and, potentially, have a negative impact on our nation's defense preparedness. Gen. Paul Gorman, the . . . retired commanding officer of the Army's Southern Command, with headquarters in Panama, told a Senate committee on June 4 [1985] that, on the contrary, such a role for the military would improve training and preparedness.

Furthermore, he directly linked the drug traffic to the funding of weapons for terrorists in Central America. In the course of questioning by Sen. Alfonse D'Amato, R.-N.Y., Gorman endorsed the Bennett amendment.

We have witnessed the largest military buildup in our nation's history, with more than $1 trillion being spent on defense in the past four years. Our Navy and Air Force have a major presence in the Caribbean and along our nation's coastline and borders. They should be assigned, at the request of civilian law-enforcement authorities, to track down and intercept drug smugglers.

Respect for the Armed Forces

Americans have great respect for the ability of the armed forces to ensure their safety and security. If given the responsibility to interdict international narcotic trafficking, the military will succeed. It should also be remembered that the military's role will be limited to points outside the land areas of the United States, where the civilian law-enforcement agencies, acting alone, have only marginal effectiveness.

The United States remains under siege, confronted by a tidal wave of drugs.

Let's use the weapons at hand. Let's commit the military to the defense of the nation by deploying our armed forces along our borders and on the high seas to interdict drugs.

II

In "Drugs—at the Source" [editorial, Aug. 4, 1986], The [Washington] Post comments that "careful, focused military-support operations" such as the one now under way in Bolivia "could help" in the war against drugs but that "important questions remain to be answered" about such efforts abroad. Those questions can and should be answered, because fighting drugs at the source is an essential part of this administration's comprehensive effort to address the narcotics problem.

As The Post notes, we as a nation have a "general reluctance" to "assign the military to a mission customarily treated as law enforcement." Reasons for that reluctance are obvious, but as a nation we also have decided to make exceptions. Legislation enacted as part of the Department of Defense Authorization Act of 1982 symbolizes public and congressional intent that the military should support civil law enforcement authorities in their efforts to halt illicit drug trafficking. The president's decision to sign the . . . National Security Decision Directive underscores our commitment to use military resources when appropriate against this insidious drug threat.

We committed the military to Operation Blast Furnace, a law enforcement effort coordinated by the Drug Enforcement Administration, after meeting two specific conditions. These are terms we must meet before any such commitment. First, we must receive an official request from the foreign government. Second, as the law requires, the secretary of defense and I must jointly determine that "an emergency circumstance" exists.

The Military Contribution

We are diligently balancing our contribution to this nation's campaign to reverse the growing drug trafficking menace with readiness implications and national security mission imperatives. In this regard, the secretary of defense . . . forwarded a list of initiatives to the National Drug Enforcement Policy Board which suggests a prudent expanded drug enforcement support role for the department as a byproduct of our primary mission activity. These options for future DoD [Department of Defense] support emphasize the most effective use of military assets for the taxpayer dollar and have the support of the Joint Chiefs of Staff.

R. Dean Tice, *Defense 86*, May/June 1986.

The law defines such an occasion. It exists only when "the size or scope of the suspected criminal activity in a given situation poses a serious threat to the interests of the United States," and when drug law enforcement "would be seriously impaired" if our assistance were not given.

A Threat to US Interests

Obviously, these are matters that require the most careful judgment based upon a conscientious review of the situation at hand. In the Bolivian instance, the judgment was made that the criminal activity at issue—the cocaine industry—does indeed pose a serious threat to our interests. More than a third of the cocaine entering the United States is grown and manufactured in Bolivia, and cocaine is a health danger to many of our citizens. Indeed, as we have been painfully reminded, it can cause death.

Just as we have a stake in protecting the life and health of all our citizens, so we also have an interest in the continued life and health of other democratic nations. The Bolivia cocaine industry threatens the . . . Bolivia democracy; as the The Post put it, in Bolivia "drugs assault the very integrity of the state."

43

The secretary of defense and I also made the judgment that without our assistance the Bolivian government would simply not be able to carry out the cocaine raids now under way. The missing element was adequate transportation for the Bolivian police. Only the U.S. military, with helicopters and support personnel, could provide the logistical capability required for this operation.

Within Limits

Once the military is committed in the drug fight abroad, it must operate within certain limits. It may not interdict or interrupt the passage of civilian vessels or aircraft. Military personnel may fire only if fired upon—in self-defense. And they may be assigned only for a specific occasion or a fixed period of time—that is, they may not be assigned indefinitely to a task. In sum, they may do what the military committed in Bolivia is now doing—providing the support necessary for a specific law enforcement effort.

Any comprehensive antidrug policy must fight drugs as close to the source as possible. Our official government policy has recognized the importance of doing this. "Careful, focused" operations such as the one in Bolivia will continue to be essential because they disrupt at an early stage the sequence of events that culminates in a person's actual consumption of illicit drugs and the often damaging consequences of that act for the individual and the community.

The administration has taken a major law enforcement step in going to Bolivia. And we are prepared to take this same step elsewhere when we are officially asked to do so and when an emergency circumstance exists.

As we pursue law enforcement strategies designed to reduce the supply of drugs, I must also emphasize, with The Post, that a government supply-side approach is by itself an insufficient answer to our nation's drug problem. All of us—in the public and private sectors alike—must find new strategies for engaging the attention of our own drug users and persuade them to reject the substances that are destroying the abilities and lives of countless Americans, and indeed imperiling the American future.

"To 'send in the Marines' . . . is insanely short-sighted."

Do Not Use Military Intervention in the War on Drugs

Bill Kauffman

Bill Kauffman is assistant editor of *Reason* magazine, a publication of the libertarian Reason Foundation which supports freedom from government control. In the following viewpoint, he expresses alarm over American use of the military in the war on drugs. Such intervention, says Kauffman, victimizes foreign peasants who have no other crops to grow, angers Latin American allies, and oversteps moral bounds.

As you read, consider the following questions:

1. Why does Kauffman conclude that enlisting the armed forces in the war on drugs, though undesirable, was inevitable?
2. According to the author, who were the real victims of the military's raid on Bolivia's cocaine trade?
3. What does the author mean when he cautions that the US will become a "Banana Republic"?

Bill Kauffman, "Join the Army, Be a Narc." Reprinted, with permission, from the December 1986 issue of REASON magazine. Copyright © 1986 by the Reason Foundation, 2716 Ocean Park Blvd., Suite 1062, Santa Monica, CA 90405.

The government's war on drugs is reaching a fittingly obscene climax. Tots betray their parents to state authorities and are rewarded for their treachery with lucrative movie offers. . . . Delaware's Pete du Pont threatens mandatory dope tests for public-school students. Otherwise sensible people are calling for drug traffickers to be put to death. (Even the Soviet Union treats its black-market capitalists better than that.)

Most ominous, though, is that the metaphorical war on drugs has been literalized. Politicians who conjure up the imagery of battle to emphasize the ardor of their cocaine-hating no longer need to feel like literary prigs; this is no wimpy Carteresque "moral equivalent of war"—it's the real thing, with soldiers and helicopters and some day, inevitably, blood.

Enlisting the armed forces in the war on drugs was, one supposes, inevitable. Militarism is the great public-works project of our day, employing well over 4 million Americans. Liberals are enamored of the government-as-employer aspect of it, while conservatives bask in the radiant glory a powerful army casts upon the nation-state. But a military really ain't much fun unless you can use it. Florida congressman Clay Shaw (R) was at least honest when, apropos the anti-drug campaign, he asked: "Why have all of those men and women and machinery and equipment, airplanes, ships, all of that talent, all of that manpower? Why keep it bottled up and suppressed and not use it?"

War Is Declared

Well, now we are using it. War is declared, and battle come down, and the site of our first major campaign in the literal war on drugs is Bolivia. The president of that desperately poor South American land, Victor Paz Estenssoro, was made to understand by his sugar daddies in Washington that the price of continued foreign aid was the surrender of national sovereignty. Paz's government was unwilling to risk losing its $50-million annual subsidy from Uncle Sam; moreover, Bolivian drug merchants were gaining political clout throughout the country. So the hemisphere's superpower was invited in.

Six Army Black Hawk helicopters and about 160 troops invaded Bolivia in July [1986], ostensibly for a 60-day operation (which has been, predictably, extended—"indefinitely"). Their mission: help Bolivia's notorious anti-drug squad, the Leopards, destroy the remote cocaine-processing laboratories.

The element of surprise was lost, thanks to Bolivian newspaper reports of the impending raids. (By contrast, the *New York Times, Washington Post,* and *Los Angeles Times* knew of the raids beforehand but withheld the information until their Bolivian brethren broke the story. The self-proclaimed independent American press didn't want to "disrupt the raid," says the *Los*

Angeles Times's Jack Nelson. Reed Irvine and other baiters of the "liberal press," take note.)

Despite the advance notice, the raids were reportedly a success. Processing labs accounting for 90 percent of Bolivia's cocaine trade have been destroyed, forcing the coke entrepreneurs to shift operations to neighboring countries or go underground for a while.

The Victims

But consider, for a moment, the true victims of this raid. Bolivia's 90,000-acre coca crop is the second-largest in the world, behind only Peru's. Its cocaine exports totaled $600 million last year—$100 million more than all legal exports combined. Tens of thousands of peasants earn their daily bread picking coca leaves.

Now there is "virtually no market for their crop," according to the Associated Press. The U.S. government has annihilated the most important industry in South America's poorest country and left a goodly portion of Bolivia's population—perhaps seven percent—without the means to support themselves. These people sure can't feed their kids on Nancy Reagan's anti-drug homilies.

Under the Guise of Fighting Drugs

Internationally, under the guise of fighting drug traffic, the government is conducting military practice and positioning for the future. . . . New ways to target immigrants. And new ways to oppose upheaval in the U.S.'s volatile "backyard." The "drug war" has been taken to places like Bolivia—U.S. Army C-5A Galaxy transport planes with Black Hawk helicopters, AWACs radar planes, M-60 machine guns, communications equipment, field kitchens and more. U.S. Attorney Rudolph Giuliani openly praised this as a "model" for the introduction of U.S. troops all over the world.

Revolutionary Worker, October 20, 1986.

Weep not, however, for Bolivian "leader" Paz. This is a superb deal for the Bolivian government. A troublesome source of domestic political opposition has disappeared. A vital (though untaxed) illegal export may be gone, but Paz will be rewarded for his complaisance. Just days after U.S. military forces invaded, the Bolivian planning minister appeared in Washington, hat in hand, begging for $100 million in economic assistance *in addition* to the $50 million U.S. taxpayers are already sending these mendicants. Just how much of this aid finds its way into the pockets of destitute peasants is a matter left to reader speculation.

Unfortunately, the Bolivian tragedy is but one example of U.S. meddling in the agricultural affairs of her smaller neighbors. A U.S.-backed marijuana-eradication campaign in Jamaica (U.S. aid,

$140 million annually) has erased 40 percent of one of that impoverished island's chief cash crops. Again, the victims are poor rural farmers, as well as members of a religious minority, the Rastafarians, who use *ganja* in their rituals.

World Narc

The U.S. government's new role as world narc is earning us the hatred of Mexicans, as well. . . . Dale Gieringer documents [in *Reason*, December 1986] the outrageous abuses of Americans' rights committed by the Drug Enforcement Administration. The DEA is no less assiduous in harassing Mexicans. Its heavy-handed meddling in Mexican police affairs has provoked a new round of anti-Americanism south of the border.

Having deprived Bolivian and Jamaican peasants of their livelihoods and whipped up nationalist resentment in Mexico, the Reagan administration is ready for new triumphs in the war on drugs. Officials are trying to use the promise of increased foreign aid to bribe the governments of Colombia, Ecuador, and Peru into surrendering their sovereignty, just as Paz has given up Bolivia's.

We are already, in Latin America, reaping the bitter fruits of past decades of military intervention to further our own ends. To "send in the Marines" all over again is insanely short-sighted.

Militarists' Thirst

Of course, the militarists' thirst is never slaked, and a large number of our statesmen are now clamoring to turn the army loose on the *American* drug trade. They hide behind the well-worn national-security fig leaf. Thunders South Carolina's Thomas Hartnett (R) of the drug menace: "This threat to national security [is] worse than any nuclear warfare or any chemical warfare waged on any battlefield." (Remember: men who are capable of saying things like this with a straight face make the laws that *you* have to live under.)

Prodded by Hartnett and legislators of similar stature, the House version of the . . . drug law contained an astonishing provision commanding the president to use the armed forces to "substantially halt the unlawful penetration of U.S. borders by aircraft and vessels carrying narcotics within 45 days." This extraordinary proposal—which called for the military to create an Iron Curtain around a free nation—passed the House easily, 237-177.

Cooler heads prevailed—including that of Defense Secretary Weinberger, who called the proposal "absurd." The provision was quietly dropped, but expect it to resurface. . . .

Siccing the military on the domestic drug trade is probably not, strictly speaking, illegal. The Posse Comitatus Act of 1878 forbids using the armed forces to execute the law, but exceptions have been made in the past, notably during riots in the 1960s. (More problematic is the legality of the Bolivian raids, which may have violated the War Powers Act of 1973.)

But beyond the legal issues lies a more basic question that the militarists ought to consider. That is, are we still a republic, with a limited government and a civilian-controlled military whose sole purpose is to defend this nation against attack; or are we to become a huge Banana Republic, where a jack-booted military acts to ensure social control at home and hemispheric hegemony abroad?

Destroying American Liberties

Bringing the Armed Forces into the business of law enforcement would destroy the historic separation of the police and armed forces, with potentially calamitous results for the liberties of Americans.

Ted Weiss, quoted in *The Village Voice*, October 21, 1986.

The grotesqueries described above certainly confirm the worst fears of the Founding Fathers, who, almost to a man, feared that a standing army could become an instrument of tyranny. James Madison spoke for his Constitutional Convention colleagues when he wrote: "Armies in time of peace are allowed on all hands to be an evil."

That is a lesson we have all too easily forgotten. The people of Bolivia are learning it the hard way, and unless the message sinks in soon, so will we.

Distinguishing Between Fact and Opinion

This activity is designed to help develop the basic reading and thinking skill of distinguishing between fact and opinion. Consider the following statement as an example: "Over one billion dollars was used to prohibit drug use and trafficking in 1985." This statement is a fact with which few people would disagree. But consider a statement which casts an opinion about drug abuse: "The federal government has not spent enough money to stop drug abuse and drug trafficking." Such a statement is clearly an expressed opinion. Many people who feel that drug abuse and trafficking must be stopped would agree, but those who do not see the drug issue as a critical problem would feel the statement is inaccurate.

When investigating controversial issues it is important that one be able to distinguish between statements of fact and statements of opinion. It is also important to recognize that not all statements of fact are true. They may appear to be true, but some are based on inaccurate or false information. For this activity, however, we are concerned with understanding the difference between those statements which appear to be factual and those which appear to be based primarily on opinion.

Most of the following statements are taken from the viewpoints in this chapter. Consider each statement carefully. *Mark O for any statement you believe is an opinion or interpretation of facts. Mark F for any statement you believe is a fact.*

If you are doing this activity as a member of a class or group, compare your answers with those of other class or group members. Be able to defend your answers. You may discover that others will come to different conclusions than you. Listening to the reasons others present for their answers may give you valuable insights in distinguishing between fact and opinion.

If you are reading this book alone, ask others if they agree with your answers. You will find this interaction valuable.

O = *opinion*
F = *fact*

1. People who use drugs aren't hurting anyone but themselves.

2. Marijuana is now one of America's principal cash crops.

3. The nation's drug use has come to be a 60-billion-a-year habit.

4. Politicians who claim to take public stands on drugs simply want to draw attention away from their habitual cowardice and incompetence.

5. There's a drug and alcohol epidemic in this country and no one is safe from its consequences.

6. Once legalized, drugs would become cheaper and more accessible to people who previously had not tried them.

7. The city of New York currently assigns eight judges to hear 20,000 narcotics cases.

8. It is generally estimated that no more than 10% of all imported drugs are actually confiscated.

9. Legalizing substances such as cocaine, marijuana, and heroin would send a message to our young people that drug use is socially acceptable and will not harm them.

10. The number of addicts of heroin and other drugs is small compared with the number of alcoholics.

11. Bolivia's cocaine exports totalled $600 million last year—$100 million more than all legal exports combined.

12. The United States remains confronted by a tidal wave of drugs.

13. The statesmen now clamoring to turn the army loose on the American drug trade are living proof that the militarists' thirst is never satisfied.

14. More than a third of the cocaine entering the United States is grown and manufactured in Bolivia.

15. The Customs Service says it intercepts only one out of every one hundred planes flying cocaine and heroin into the country.

Periodical Bibliography

The following articles have been selected to supplement the diverse views expressed in this chapter.

Peter B. Bensinger	"An Inadequate War Against Drugs," *Newsweek*, July 28, 1986.
Joseph A. Califano Jr.	"A Natural Attack on Addiction Is Long Overdue," *The New York Times*, September 15, 1986.
Hodding Carter III	"Keep Costs of Illegal Drug Use in Perspective," *The Wall Street Journal*, August 14, 1986.
Alexander Cockburn	"Some Radical Notions About Fighting Drugs," *The Wall Street Journal*, September 11, 1986.
Richard C. Cowan	"How the Narcs Created Crack," *National Review*, December 5, 1986.
Harper's	"Forum: What Is Our Drug Problem?" December 1985.
Edward I. Koch	"Declaring War on Drugs," *Conservative Digest*, August 1985.
Chris Lutes	"Positive Peer Pressure: A New Weapon Against Drugs," *Christianity Today*, February 20, 1987.
Cait Murphy	"High Times in America: Why Our Drug Policy Can't Work," *Policy Review*, Winter 1987.
Mitchell S. Rosenthal	"Time for a Real War on Drugs," *Newsweek*, September 2, 1985.
Evan Thomas	"America's Crusade: What Is Behind the Latest War on Drugs," *Time*, September 15, 1986.
James Wall	"Antidrug Bandwagon Promises a Quick Fix," *Christian Century*, October 8, 1986.
Ellen Willis	"A Few Words in Defense of Drugs . . . And a Few Reservations," *The Village Voice*, January/February 1987.
Tom Zambito	"The Inside Dope: Communities Are Winning the War Against Drugs," *Policy Review*, Fall 1985.

Are International Drug Campaigns Effective?

Chapter Preface

Most illegal drugs consumed in the United States come from outside the country. The federal government has spent several billion dollars trying to stop these drugs from crossing US borders, but its efforts have been hampered by the complex system of narcotics trafficking, the allure of enormous profits, and the lack of cooperation from foreign governments.

In nations such as Mexico, Bolivia, Jamaica, Pakistan, and Burma, drugs are a major part of the national export incomes. The growers, the traffickers, the distributing organizations, and the dealers make substantial profits from sales to American consumers. The governments may benefit overtly or covertly from this booming industry and thus are reluctant to crack down on the drug trade in their countries.

The United States' wish to end the drug trade is often at odds with its efforts to promote positive foreign relations with the countries involved. For example, the US has, in some instances, threatened to withhold economic assistance to debt-burdened countries until these countries agree to eradicate their narcotics crops. Proponents believe that this kind of pressure can significantly reduce available narcotics. Others believe that, in reality, little impact is made on international drug trafficking and that the US creates more enemies by forcing foreign governments to wipe out their citizens' one sure cash crop.

Thus the controversy over the international drug campaign becomes a clash between those who want to eliminate drug trafficking and those who want to maintain good foreign relations. The debate will continue as long as the nation's foreign obligations and its domestic priorities remain at odds.

"Our diplomatic and program efforts . . . are improving the prospects of narcotics control."

US Efforts To Stop Drug Trafficking Have Been Successful

George P. Shultz

George P. Shultz is the US secretary of state. In the following address given before the Miami Chamber of Commerce, Secretary Shultz enumerates the successes of the government's international narcotics control campaign. According to Shultz, the Reagan administration has overcome many obstacles in fighting drug production and trafficking and will continue to do so.

As you read, consider the following questions:

1. What examples does the author give to prove that international narcotics control has been successful?
2. According to the author, what obstacles prevent the US from reducing crop production in other countries?
3. What four basic principles of international narcotics policy does Shultz list?

George P. Shultz, "The Campaign Against Drugs: The International Dimension," *Department of State Bulletin*, November 1984.

You are all aware of what this Administration has been doing to address the domestic aspects of our drug problem. The First Lady has made it her personal crusade to educate our youth on the dangers of drugs, and Nancy Reagan's valiant efforts have given great impetus to this dimension of national prevention. Vice President Bush has played the leading role in improving our domestic drug interdiction efforts. . . . He is the head of the South Florida Task Force, and he is also the head of the National Narcotics Border Interdiction System. These and other efforts have shown encouraging results on the domestic side of the problem. It should be clear that demand helps create supply, and we cannot expect to meet the challenge of drug abuse without doing all we can to reduce the demand for drugs here at home.

The International Dimension

It is equally clear, however, that we cannot meet the challenge of drug abuse here at home without also attacking the worldwide network of narcotics production and trafficking. I want you to know that drug abuse is not only a top priority for this Administration's domestic policy, it is a top priority in our foreign policy as well.

Every year, drug traffickers smuggle into this country 4 metric tons of heroin; as much as 70 metric tons of cocaine; and as much as 15,000 metric tons of marijuana. These drugs come from all over the world: from Colombia, Peru, Bolivia, Mexico, Belize, Jamaica, Pakistan, Afghanistan, Iran, Thailand, and Burma. Once the crops are produced in these countries, they are often shipped elsewhere for processing and then in their refined narcotic form are shipped again to local suppliers in Western Europe, the United States, and throughout the industrialized world. Drug money is laundered in international financial markets. Middlemen are hired to smuggle the drugs past customs officials and the Coast Guard. It is a smooth and ever more efficient operation that is truly an international effort. . . .

Novel problems require fresh thinking, new tools, and new approaches. You have my personal pledge that the Department of State is committed to this effort. We have been working closely with Federal drug enforcement agencies on new ways of dealing with the growing narcotics problem on an international level. And we do so not only to fight the calamity of domestic drug abuse but to fight the growing threat of international lawlessness as well.

Meeting the Challenge

To meet the challenge of international narcotics trafficking requires, above all, international cooperation between those nations that share our concern about this growing threat to our societies.

During this Administration, we have gone beyond all previous efforts to promote international cooperation on narcotics control. In September 1981, President Reagan laid out our objectives. He called for "a foreign policy that vigorously seeks to interdict and eradicate illicit drugs, wherever cultivated, processed, or transported." American officials at the highest levels—including President Reagan, Vice President Bush, and myself, our ambassadors and senior State Department officials—have continually emphasized to foreign leaders the importance we attach to their cooperation on the narcotics issue. We have placed our greatest emphasis on reaching bilateral agreements on crop control, eradication, and interdiction with nations where narcotics are produced, shipped, and consumed. We have also worked hard in the United Nations to support international efforts to stem the flow of drugs and reduce production.

Gaining Control

Because of the severity and complexity of the narcotics problems, some people say that the situation is hopeless. Nothing could be further from the truth. Recent events give reason to be optimistic that the current approaches of the international community are making significant progress in establishing the base for potential control of production and distribution of major illicit substances. I choose these words carefully; we do not have control, but we have improved the possibility that we will gain control.

Jon R. Thomas, *Department of State Bulletin*, January 1985.

Many nations, concerned as we are with the drug problem, have taken significant steps. In Colombia, an aerial herbicide eradication program that began July 5 [1984] has destroyed more than 4,200 acres of marijuana, a truly major breakthrough in the global control effort. This initial effort alone could keep nearly $3-billion worth of marijuana off our streets—and the Colombian program has just started. In Peru, despite the threat of terrorism, authorities have eradicated nearly 5,000 acres of coca bushes used to produce cocaine; in fact, the government has . . . sent its military forces into the coca-growing region. We are working with other South American governments to prevent the spread of drug production into new source areas.

Examples of Success

In Asia, the Government of Pakistan continues to extend its ban on cultivation of opium poppy into additional areas of the Northwest Frontier Province, and it has reported sharply increased seizures of heroin in the first quarter of 1984. And [in November, 1984] . . . , Pakistani officials seized 163 kilograms of opium and

57

20 kilograms of heroin in one raid on a heroin laboratory. The Thai Government has increased its commitment to controlling opium cultivation in villages that receive development assistance and moved aggressively against the opium warlords. The Burmese Government is exploring with us more systematic methods of eradication. . . .

We know the difficulties involved in reducing crop production. In many producer countries, narcotics production is or has become an important fact of everyday life. There are parts of the world where opium and coca are used as part of centuries-old traditions, and, of course, many nations have growing addiction problems of their own which encourage narcotics production. Finally, many producer countries are just too poor to mount effective crop control and eradication programs.

Our international narcotics policies are aimed at overcoming these obstacles. We are providing bilateral assistance . . . to 18 governments whose expertise or resources are insufficient to meet the challenge of crop reduction. We have encouraged multilateral assistance through the UN Fund for Drug Abuse Control and other international organizations. The Department of State has worked with the U.S. Drug Enforcement Administration, the Customs Service, and the Coast Guard to provide training to foreign governments in narcotics control, enforcement, and interdiction. Since 1971, we have provided funds to train more than 25,000 foreign enforcement officers. . . . We have also tried to help foreign governments alert their publics to the threat that drug abuse poses to their societies. . . .

Significant Strides

The hurdles we face in confronting this problem are many, but we have made significant strides in recent years. Our international narcotics policy has rested on four basic principles:

First, countries where narcotics are produced or through which drugs are shipped must accept their responsibilities under international treaties to reduce crops and interdict drug smuggling.

Second, the international community must assist those nations that lack the resources to take the necessary steps.

Third, worldwide emphasis must be on crop control and eradication—we have seen that interdiction alone is not the answer.

Fourth, in producer nations that need our help, our narcotics-related economic assistance must be linked to agreements on reducing crop levels.

Our goal must be to control narcotics production in all geographic areas simultaneously. We have learned the hard way that markets shift to meet demand; we cannot focus on only a few areas at a time. When we helped reduce heroin production in Turkey, for example, increased production in Mexico filled the gap. A truly international effort aimed at all producer nations is essential. And we are moving down that path.

In 1981, when this Administration took office, we had commitments to work on reducing narcotics crops from Burma, Turkey, and Mexico. Today, thanks to this Administration's efforts and to the growing concern of leaders in producer countries, we also have commitments from Pakistan, Colombia, Belize, Peru, and Bolivia. In Pakistan, the world's leading supplier of heroin, we have seen tremendous results. Thanks in part to the extraordinary efforts of the Pakistani Government and to U.S. assistance, raw opium production has been reduced from a massive 800 metric tons per year in 1979 to under 60 metric tons per year in 1983. Mexico's production of processed heroin, once as high as 7.5 metric tons per year, was reduced to 1.4 metric tons in 1983.

A Long Way To Go

Much has been done, and we are only beginning the fight. Obviously, we still have a long way to go. Some countries have not done enough to reduce their crop levels. Others could do more to curb the flow of narcotics through their territory and airspace and end their use as a way station by drug traffickers. We must seek greater cooperation and increased effectiveness in reducing cultivation in all of the producer nations. Overall crop production still provides a surplus of narcotics that greatly exceeds not only American but worldwide demand.

An Effective Strategy

We believe we have a sound strategy, and it is not only working but increasingly effective. . . . There are congressional reports which offer a conflicting view. We agree with some aspects of these reports but note numerous inaccuracies as well. I think the salient aspect of these reports is that they virtually concede that there is really no alternative but to negotiate crop control programs that can be simultaneously effective in all growing regions. That, in fact, is the objective we have pursued. And the data available show that this strategy is beginning to bring down production.

Jon R. Thomas, *Department of State Bulletin*, June 1985.

And we know that the international narcotics network is larger, more efficient, and more sophisticated than ever before. The narcotics market is an ever-shifting phenomenon that adapts to each new method we devise to confront it. Drug smugglers have managed to find new ways of smuggling to elude our stepped-up efforts. Finally, we have seen that some communist nations continue to use the drug trade for their own purposes and, therefore, have an interest in its perpetuation. The international drug problem, therefore, presents an increasing challenge to our intelligence community to provide good estimates of narcotics production and to trace the links between drugs, terrorism, and communist insurgencies.

But we are making progress. We have a policy in place that addresses all aspects of the international problem—the cultivation, production, and distribution of drugs, the flow of profits, the impacts upon other countries as well as our own. And we have developed broad-based international support for controlling the narcotics trade.

I believe that our diplomatic and program efforts, together with the increasing awareness in producer countries of the disastrous effects on them of the drug trade, are improving the prospects of narcotics control.

---

*"There is plenty of evidence that U.S. foreign
drug control efforts have been unsuccessful."*

US Efforts To Stop
Drug Trafficking Have
Failed

Peter Reuter

Peter Reuter is a senior economist at the Rand Corporation in
Washington, DC. In the following viewpoint, he describes international drug trafficking and gives several reasons why the US
cannot stop it. According to Reuter, until foreign farmers find
something else to grow, drug traffickers will continue shipping
narcotics to the US.

As you read, consider the following questions:

1. According to Reuter, why do US efforts to reduce crop
   production in other countries fail?
2. Why does the author believe US policies will not affect
   drug consumption in the US?
3. Why, after all his criticisms, does the author support some
   type of international drug production control?

Peter Reuter, "Eternal Hope: America's Quest for Narcotics Control." Reprinted with
permission of the author from: THE PUBLIC INTEREST, No. 79 (Spring 1985), pp. 79-95.
© 1985 by National Affairs, Inc.

Throughout the twentieth century, the government of the United States has maintained that the solution to the American drug abuse problem lies with the foreign nations that produce the most important illicit drugs. This has been the view of administrations as different as John Kennedy's and Ronald Reagan's and it has been held about drugs as different as heroin and marijuana. The tone of the official statements on this matter has become somewhat less accusatory over the years—the government no longer suspects Communist governments of attempting to corrupt American moral fiber and fighting power through drug exports, though the Bulgarians, North Koreans, and Cubans have in fact been caught in minor facilitating roles from time to time. But there has been no change in the view that cutting exports from countries such as Burma, Colombia, and Pakistan is the best method for reducing U.S. consumption of heroin, cocaine, and marijuana. As the White House stated in 1982, "elimination of illegal drugs at or near their foreign source is the most effective means to reduce the domestic supply of these substances."

This notion became a genuine part of American foreign policy when President Nixon, under heavy congressional pressure, initiated a series of bilateral agreements with source countries to assist them in reducing their exports. These agreements have become a standard component of battles between the State Department and Congress, Congress generally charging that the Department gives too little high-level attention to the drug problem. But there is no political dispute about the centrality of these international programs to American drug policy. The only dispute concerns the appropriate levels of expenditure and the intensity of pressure to be exerted on other nations.

The notion of production control, as it is usually called, is indeed an appealing one: Enough of the band-aids of interdiction and domestic law enforcement; we shall strike at the *fundamentals*, namely drug production itself. I think it fair to say that the appeal is peculiarly strong for Americans. The rest of the world is much more resigned to band-aids, if not to the ailment itself.

Unsuccessful Efforts

Unfortunately, there is plenty of evidence that U.S. foreign drug control efforts have been unsuccessful. In recent years, U.S. consumption and world production appear to have increased somewhat for heroin, and greatly for the other two drugs; prices have been declining in the United States.

The failures of U.S. international programs are not the result of incompetence or inadequate resources; they are inherent in the structure of the problem. The producer countries jointly lack either the motivation or the means to reduce total production. Even if such reduction were possible, it is unlikely that U.S. im-

62

ports from each of these countries, apart from Mexico and Turkey, would be affected. Just as important, the set of source countries is readily expandable. The international programs serve a useful function in curbing illicit drug use in some major source countries. But they will do little to reduce drug abuse in the United States. . . .

Ed Gamble. Reprinted with permission.

The U.S. has tried a number of approaches. Some efforts focus on production itself. Resources are provided to aid local law enforcement agencies to eradicate crops, either through the spraying of a herbicide (as was done in Mexico for opium poppies) or by manually uprooting plants (as is occasionally done with coca plants in Peru). A number of projects have been funded, either by the United States directly or through multilateral agencies (such as the United Nations Fund for Drug Abuse Control), that aim at providing alternative commercial crops for farmers growing coca (in Peru) or poppies (in Burma). . . .

Many Impediments

Despite the increasing concern with local drug use, there are many impediments to successful crop reduction efforts in producer countries. The first is that farmers usually do not have an easy alternative commercial crop. Currently, poppies may indeed be the only crop that can be produced in remote areas of Burma and Thailand to provide steady cash income. Everyone recognizes that increased law enforcement efforts against farmers will have little effect unless other productive opportunities are provided. This takes many years. The basic strategy of the UN Fund for Drug Abuse Control (UNFDAC) and the Thai government is to develop these alternative cash crops.

In most cases, this requires, among other things, the creation of a new infrastructure (roads in particular) to permit the efficient delivery of bulkier and more perishable crops to distant markets. Farmers must also learn how to produce crops entirely new to their regions, such as cacao in the Upper Huallaga valley of Peru and kidney beans in the Chiang Mai area of Thailand. Whether these efforts will turn out to be sufficient is a matter of speculation. (Indeed, subsidized irrigation and fertilizer might have the perverse effect of increasing the productivity of illicit farming.) The programs in Thailand show promise but encompass a population of only a few thousand, and there are no instances in which crop substitution has actually been achieved on a large scale. . . .

Weak Control

A second major obstacle to crop reduction is the generally weak control of governments in the producing areas. The Thai and Burmese governments have long been fighting insurgent movements in the hills that are home to the poppy growers. The Peruvian government has little effective control in some of the very remote regions that produce coca leaves. Similar statements are true for Afghanistan, Pakistan, Bolivia, and Laos, at least. Even where governments are strongly motivated and have sensible plans, they are likely to have great difficulty in implementing them.

Third, some major source countries, notably Iran and Afghanistan, have hostile relations with the United States. Though they may adopt policies to reduce domestic consumption, they are unconcerned about U.S. imports. Fourth, U.S. relations with most of the other countries involved in opium production are very complex. The United States would like Pakistan to adopt certain policies with respect to Afghanistan. It seeks to retain bases in Thailand. It would like Colombia to take particular positions with respect to Central America. A DEA [Drug Enforcement Administration] official explaining the relatively light pressure being exerted on Jamaica was quoted in the *New York Times* as saying, "Some analysts believe that if you came in with a severe narcotics program, you could affect the existence of the present government . . . Drugs are a serious problem. But communism is a greater problem." Given all these considerations, and the disinclination of diplomats and policymakers to concern themselves with such unseemly matters as the drug trade, it is difficult to put consistent pressure on source country governments.

Finally, and perhaps most important, the set of producer countries is not fixed. New producers emerge all the time. . . . There is no reason to believe that other countries, with large impoverished peasant populations and weak central governments, would not soon become significant producers if the current producers greatly cut back. A large or traditional local market turns out not to be essential. In the instance of marijuana, we must also note the rapid growth of very high quality domestic U.S. supplies. . . .

Lack of Progress

Congress has been frequently indignant about the lack of progress in curtailing foreign production and exports to the U.S. Statutory restrictions have been placed on U.S. aid to those nations involved in drug production, but it has been difficult to implement these restrictions. The complexity of U.S. relations with most other nations, as well as the difficulty of determining just how seriously these foreign governments are in fact taking the problem, have combined to prevent effective use of other aid programs to encourage crop reduction overseas. Only one country has ever been denied aid as a consequence of its failure to cut back drug production: In late 1980, aid to the corrupt Bolivian regime of General Garcia Meza was suspended, to be resumed in 1983 following the election of President Siles Zuazo.

A Painful Truth

It's time someone spoke aloud a painful truth. Our government has invested massive manpower and millions of dollars in anti-drug enforcement efforts that may only have made the problem worse.

Lionel Van Deerlin, *The San Diego Tribune*, January 23, 1986.

Official documents—the 1982 White House *Drug Strategy*, the 1984 INM [International Narcotics Matters] report to Congress—say all the right things. There are no illusions about the will and power of most of the relevant governments. It is noted that the United States is not on friendly terms with some of the critical producer countries. There is an awareness that the problem for individual countries is a long-term one; peasant farmers are understandably unconcerned about American drug use and are likely to be rather more efficient at opium, marijuana or coca production than at producing other, newer crops. But documents continue to advocate the same strategies—treaties, crop replacement, and so on.

It is unlikely that such policies will be successful in reducing American drug consumption. They ignore the realities of the world drug market. Many countries are sources for U.S. consumption, and exports to this country are affected at most only slightly by their total production. (In the case of Mexican opium, U.S. efforts were able to reduce total production so substantially that there was simply too little heroin to deliver. But Mexico is distinct from most major source countries: the absence of an indigenous market meant that there was no local consumption base from which to bid for export material.)

In general, if it is the cost of distribution that determines a nation's exports to the United States, then two consequences must be noted. First, INM programs should focus on those countries that are the major sources for U.S. markets, not those that are simply the largest producers. There has already been some implicit recognition of this; the attention given to Mexico represented its importance to U.S. consumption, not to world production. Second, except where U.S. consumption is the bulk of the market, programs should focus on distribution to a greater extent than they do. Unfortunately, we have little idea of how to make distribution a more risky and expensive activity in other countries.

International Control Program

There are, despite this, good arguments for maintaining an international production control program. First, some success cannot be ruled out. The right set of ecological and political events might make it possible, through effective diplomacy, to cause a major short-term disruption in the U.S. drug market. For example, a drought in Afghanistan, continued success in crop substitution in Pakistan, and the installation of a more authoritarian regime in Thailand might make heroin somewhat scarce in the United States for two or three years, this being a good guess as to the time needed to increase production elsewhere and to establish the necessary trafficking routes. Estimates of the annual social cost of drug abuse in the United States are highly speculative, but a figure in the tens of billions is not unreasonable. Spending a few million dollars annually for even a 1 percent probability of reducing that cost by $10 billion or so is not unwise.

Second, the vast array of international treaties that attempt to restrict the diversion of licit production into illicit markets is worth preserving. Note here an important distinction between the U.S. and the source countries: Because the U.S. is wealthy and populated with recent immigrants from many different countries, it has relatively smoothly functioning traffic flows to a number of producer countries. That is not true for many of the source countries themselves. A drying-up of heroin supplies in Bangkok is unlikely to bring a flow of drugs to Thailand from Pakistan, let alone Mexico. Consequently, the major beneficiary of U.S. efforts at curtailing Thai drug production is Thailand itself, along with other countries in the region (most notably Malaysia, whose drug users are dependent on Thai opium). The U.S. commitment to reducing illicit production is important in these regions. Its abandonment might greatly increase the availability of drugs for illicit markets throughout the world, the social costs of which, for the source countries, are likely to be substantial.

Congressional Rhetoric

These are arguments for maintaining the existing programs. They are also arguments for lowering the level of rhetoric, particularly in Congress, concerning the importance of these programs in helping deal with the domestic drug abuse problem. They are best seen as part of America's general foreign aid policy. They should be seen only secondarily as (very speculative) investments in the long-term reduction of the availability of drugs in the U.S.

"These governments know they could lose all U.S. assistance if they fail to take adequate steps to cooperate . . . on narcotics control."

Pressure on Foreign Governments Will Stop Drug Trafficking

John C. Whitehead

John C. Whitehead is the US deputy secretary of state. In the following statement, made before the Subcommittee on Foreign Operations of the Senate Appropriations Committee, he supports US pressure on foreign governments to eliminate drug trafficking. According to Whitehead, foreign governments will work harder to stop drug production in their own countries if the US links economic assistance to narcotics control. If fewer drugs are produced, reasons Whitehead, fewer illegal substances will wind up on American streets.

As you read, consider the following questions:

1. According to Whitehead, what is the government's most effective tool in controlling narcotics trafficking?
2. What reasons does the author give for being encouraged about the progress of narcotics control?
3. What examples does the author give of how US assistance and narcotics control are linked?

John C. Whitehead before the Subcommittee of Foreign Operation of the Senate Appropriations Committee in Washington, DC on August 14, 1986. In Current Policy No. 863, published by the US Department of State, Bureau of Public Affairs.

International narcotics control is central to the pursuit of our foreign policy objectives. We have and will continue to use every opportunity to convey the message to our friends in the international community on the need for greater effort in controlling narcotics traffic.

The most effective tool we have in this effort is the growing realization among foreign governments that narcotics trafficking is not just an American problem, but a universal threat. The efforts of the First Lady and our high-level attention to this problem are already paying dividends. Countries in which narcotics are produced or which are part of the international trafficking pattern now recognize the unacceptably high risk that narcotics pose to their own societies. These risks range from increases in violent crime to national security threats by narcoterrorist groups. The international community is finally recognizing the challenge we all face. That is the first and most important step in winning the battle.

Nevertheless, there remains a large and unacceptable gap between perception and effective action. We expect more concrete measures from our friends and are prepared to encourage and support them. The situation remains serious. . . .

Continued Pressure

We still have a long way to go. I would not minimize the obstacles, but I am heartened by what I believe are clearly positive trends. I believe that our friends recognize the need to eliminate this scourge. They know that we mean business. Continued and increased pressure has to be applied at all points of the chain— through crop control; through increased seizures of both drug products and financial assets; through intensified investigation and prosecution of traffickers; and through effective treatment and prevention of drug abuse. . . .

Of the 18 countries that are the primary sources of illicit narcotics entering the United States, 15 receive some form of U.S. economic, military, or narcotics control assistance. Fourteen of the fifteen conducted eradication programs in 1985; the other, Morocco, relies on interdiction to control hashish production. The remaining three—Iran, Afghanistan, and Laos—are politically inaccessible to us.

Security assistance levels are significant in 11 of the 14 cases. However, narcotics assistance constituted all of the assistance ($700,000) to Brazil and 98% of the $10.3 million given to Mexico, while Venezuela's total assistance was $100,000 in military training funds.

Beyond these source countries, there are other nations which are important transit points for illicit narcotics shipments to the United States, such as India, Malaysia, the Bahamas, Lebanon, and Turkey. Of these, all but the Bahamas receive some economic or military assistance.

There are both direct and indirect links between U.S. assistance and narcotics control.

The countries in which narcotics control and development assistance objectives have been most closely linked are Peru, Bolivia, and Pakistan. In each country, AID [Agency for International Development] and INM [International Narcotic Matters] have agreed on target areas, and development assistance is conditioned on achieving specific narcotics control objectives. For example, much of the development assistance intended for the Chapare region of Bolivia, the primary growing region for coca destined to become cocaine, has not been spent since 1983 because its release is contingent upon Bolivia complying with conditions of its 1983 agreement with the United States.

Applying Force

Ninety-five percent of the world's cocaine . . . originates in only two countries, Peru and Bolivia. They have a combined population approximately equal to that of California. They are impoverished and desperately in need of aid. Surely, it would be relatively easy to encourage—and, if necessary, to force—those countries to stop growing coca.

James Mills, *The New York Times*, September 5, 1986.

There are various types of indirect links between control and development assistance, such as the poppy clauses used in Pakistan and Thailand. These clauses commit a government to keeping specific development areas free of narcotics, especially areas which have not been traditional narcotics growing areas. In the one instance when new opium poppy was discovered in an area of Pakistan which was under such an agreement, the government destroyed the crop.

AID and INM emphasize development assistance, rather than crop substitution, to control narcotics. That change in policy reflects the discovery that, under substitution programs, farmers grew new crops but didn't abandon opium poppy.

The Model Will Work

Despite the disappointment in the spring 1986 opium crop, which expanded largely in response to greatly increased demand and higher prices within the region, it still appears that the model developed by INM in Pakistan works there and will work elsewhere. Specific kinds of development assistance in selected areas are conditioned on assurances—backed up by demonstrable enforcement—that the areas will be rid of illicit narcotics crops. For example, Thailand has a program in which development assistance is conditioned upon entire villages agreeing to keep their farming areas free of poppy. Since 1984, that program has steadily progressed—boosted in 1985 and 1986 by the Thai Army's aggressive new eradication program.

So far, assistance that is directly or indirectly linked to narcotics control through one or more types of agreements has been discussed. Other types of assistance are not tied to control, such as most military assistance, and economic assistance to nongrowing areas. However, the government of every source and transit nation is fully aware of the conditions imposed in Public Law 98-164. Without exception, these governments know they could lose all U.S. assistance if they fail to take adequate steps to cooperate with the U.S. government on narcotics control.

> *"No foreign government can do much for, or to, the U.S. drug problem."*

Pressure on Foreign Governments Is Useless

Mark Kleiman

Mark Kleiman was director of policy analysis in the Criminal Division of the Justice Department early in the Reagan administration. He is now researching drug policy at Harvard University. In the following viewpoint, Kleiman lists his "rogue's gallery" of foreign governments involved in, or tolerant of, narcotics trafficking. According to Kleiman, it is naive of the US government to think that pressure on these foreign governments will stop the drug trade. Also, he adds, it is wrong to discriminately pressure unfriendly governments and merely slap the hands of friendly ones.

As you read, consider the following questions:

1. According to Kleiman, why are so many governments involved in drug trafficking?
2. What evidence does the author give that the US government's treatment of foreign countries is hypocritical?
3. What, according to the author, is the truth about the foreign drug trade?

Mark Kleiman, "We Can't Stop Friend or Foe in the Drug Trade," *The Wall Street Journal*, April 9, 1985. Reprinted with the author's permission.

The State Department seems to want us to believe that the U.S. drug problem is largely the fault of communist governments and movements that traffic in drugs to make money while weakening the American social fabric. Various congressmen, on the other hand, want to know why the administration has refused to enforce the law that denies U.S. aid and trade concessions to nations failing to act against drug exports when the governments involved are on our side in the Cold War.

There is less to all of this than meets the eye.

Governments, their agencies, their employees and their foreign surrogates are rather frequently involved in drug dealing, because:

- It is a way to make quick, substantial and untraceable money.
- They often need or want money they don't have to account for.
- They have powers, resources, immunities and organizational capabilities that give them advantages in some aspects of drug dealing, and these make them more competitive in moving narcotics than they are in making steel or automobiles.

A Partial Rogue's Gallery

Even governments that do not traffic in drugs can help drug dealing in other ways, either by failing—corruptly, negligently or through incapacity—to prevent production and export of drugs or by creating havens of banking and corporate secrecy, thus helping drug dealers handle their money without getting caught.

None of this is any respecter of ideology. A (very) partial rogue's gallery would have pictures of:

- Bulgarian customs guards reselling seized heroin.
- Colombian colonels protecting marijuana exports.
- Left-wing Colombian M-19 guerrillas financed with cocaine money.
- Right-wing Colombian death squads financed with cocaine money.
- Cayman Islands (U.K.) banking authorities enforcing banking-secrecy laws to conceal drug dealers' assets.
- Afghan mujaheddin growing poppies and selling opium to buy guns.
- The Kuomintang (before 1949) and to this day various Kuomintang "lost armies" in Burma making a living from poppy growing and heroin refining.
- The North Korean diplomatic service financing its embassies by smuggling heroin in diplomatic pouches.
- Anti-Communist Hmong irregulars during the war in Vietnam supporting themselves—with the help of planes from the CIA-backed Air America—by dealing in opium and heroin.
- The Nugan Hand bank (which, if not actually an arm of the U.S. intelligence community, at least had close ties to elements of it) financing heroin deals through Hong Kong.

Ed Gamble. Reprinted with permission.

• The Iranian government conferring retroactive diplomatic immunity on a nephew of the Ayatollah Khomeini caught with a kilogram of heroin in West Germany.

• The Hungarian pharmaceutical industry shipping bulk methaqualone powder under bogus end-use certificates to Colombia to be pressed into counterfeit Quaaludes for the U.S. market.

Other Governments Involved

Other governments implicated in the trade, at least through inaction, include: Pakistan, the Bahamas, Bolivia, the Turks and Caicos Islands, Nicaragua and Mexico. Nor is it only foreign governments that find it difficult to control their law-enforcement machinery: In asking about the role of Mexican police agencies in the death of a U.S. drug agent there, we should not forget our own police and drug homicide scandals in Miami and Puerto Rico.

Among U.S. domestic political groups, both the Rastafarians (a Jamaican religious cult that employs the ritual use of marijuana) and the anti-Castro Omega-7 movement have used drug dealing as a means of support.

Most everyone wants to crack down on drug dealing (except for those libertarians who take their ideology without ice or water). In consequence, when governments tire of accusing each other of torture, murder, genocide and Sabbath-breaking, they call each

74

other dope dealers. It is the one unanswerable charge; even torture, murder and genocide (under euphemisms) have their
defenders, but every man's hand is against the pusher.

US Hypocrisy

When unfriendly governments and movements (those unfriendly to us and those to whom we have decided to be unfriendly) are involved in drug dealing, the issue is trumpeted, as
in the indictment of a sitting minister of the Cuban government.
Similar behavior by friendly governments and movements is
handled quietly; we did finally ask for the extradition of a member
of the Argentinian military government, but only after Raul Alfon-
sin's election as civilian president.

The Drug Enforcement Administration and intelligence-
community reports implicating unfriendly governments become
the basis of congressional testimony. Similar reports about friendly
governments are marked "Top Secret." Nor can this really be called
an abuse of the classification system; it would, in fact, damage
U.S. security interests to publish the fact that the government of
X, whose troops we are training to bait the Bear, is up to its medals
in the drug trade or the money-laundering business, and that the
U.S. government says so.

It is fashionable to say that we should put more pressure on
foreign governments to stop the drug trade. This raises three questions: Would the pressure be successful? If so, would there be any
effect on our drug problem? What other interests would we have
to sacrifice? In my view, the answers are, respectively: probably
not in most cases, almost certainly not, and, far more than we
would care to.

Our influence with foreign governments is a scarce resource to
be economized. Even ignoring foreign policy, and even from a
strictly selfish point of view, we probably have a stronger interest
in the farm policies, per-capita rates of gross national product and
public-health measures of most foreign governments than we have
in their drug exports. Better that Mexico should ship us more oil
than less marijuana. Haiti's thugs in uniform and thieves in office
threaten U.S. interests far more profoundly than do Jamaica's
government-tolerated drug producers and smugglers. Who would
seriously propose cutting off arms to Afghanistan until the freedom
fighters stop growing opium?

A US Problem

Drug enforcement and drug-abuse prevention can be useful tools
of foreign policy when they serve the needs of a foreign government or help political forces friendly to us. But the U.S. drug problem has to be solved in this country, with enforcement, prevention and treatment.

The Harrison Narcotics Act of 1914 didn't repeal the law of

supply and demand. There are so many potential sources that the drugs are going to come from somewhere, and the import price of drugs is so low as a fraction of final consumer price that foreign actions won't make drugs significantly more expensive.

The typical "victory" in the foreign-source control program remains the Mexican marijuana eradication program. Spraying the herbicide Paraquat on Mexican marijuana fields virtually eliminated Mexico as a source of marijuana for the U.S. market, less by destroying the crops than by scaring the users. Almost immediately, Colombian production rose to fill the empty market niche, and U.S. marijuana markets were disrupted minimally, if at all.

Telling the Truth

The only major exception to the rule that no foreign government can do much for, or to, the U.S. drug problem, involves Mexican poppy production, and the Mexicans have been pretty good about that.

Virtually Impossible

It is very difficult to convince a foreign government to take the serious political and economic risks that are entailed by an all-out campaign against, say, cocaine production when the American public's predilection for cocaine is so well-known. And it is virtually impossible to persuade foreign growers of marijuana to stop producing when one American in four has tried the drug—and billions of dollars in profits are being made by marijuana growers in the United States.

Mathea Falco, *The New York Times Magazine*, December 11, 1983.

If all this is true, should the U.S. continue to use the narcotics issue one-sidedly as an anti-communist propaganda weapon, as it now does with human rights? This partly depends on your view about the relationship between diplomacy and veracity, and partly on whether you think the drug issue appeals to important audiences abroad. If, as seems likely, the issue is only good for domestic consumption, my answer would be "probably not."

The responsibility of the media and academics is more straightforward: to tell as much of the truth as possible to whoever will listen. The truth is that, on balance, our enemies are no deeper in the drug trade than are our friends, and the whole thing doesn't matter nearly as much as some people think it does.

"The new antidrug alliances are . . . important in inter-American politics."

Narcotics Control Has Improved Foreign Relations

Elliott Abrams

Elliott Abrams is the US Assistant Secretary for Inter-American Affairs. In the following statement, made before the Council on Foreign Relations in New York City, he presents evidence of cooperation on narcotics control between the US and foreign governments. According to Abrams, most Latin American countries responsible for drug production have willingly joined the United States in its war on drugs. The most effective policy, he says, is to help these governments as much as possible, for in their hands lie solutions to the drug problem.

As you read, consider the following questions:

1. According to Abrams, why has there been a dramatic change in international cooperation over narcotics control? What examples does he give of this cooperation?
2. Why does the author advocate more help for foreign countries who are working against the drug trade? What kind of help does he suggest?

Elliott Abrams, "Drug Wars: The New Alliance Against Traffickers and Terrorists," *Department of State Bulletin*, April 1986.

Not very long ago, the discussion of drug trafficking consisted mostly of finger pointing. We blamed Latin Americans for indifference to the production and movement of narcotics northward. And they pointed to the United States and its insatiable market as the cause of that traffic. Within our own government, different agencies belittled each other's efforts, and some even claimed that fighting narcotics would "degrade" their mission and should best be left to traditional local and federal law enforcement officials, the "narcs."

There has been a dramatic change. There is a bit of the "narc" in all of us now—from presidents of Latin American democracies, to commanders of U.S. Navy destroyers in the Caribbean, to Assistant Secretaries of State for Inter-American Affairs. There is, of course, still plenty of blame to be laid. . . . But a significant story of the 1980s in this hemisphere, ourselves very much included, has been the breaking down of old attitudes and jealousies, the upgrading of missions, and precedent-setting cooperation against the traffickers and their guerrilla allies and protectors.

In Washington, the level and productivity of joint narcotics control ventures among government agencies is making bureaucratic history. In exactly the same way, effective cooperation among the Andean countries of South America and Brazil is confounding historical judgments about narrow nationalism and the "traditional" role of the military and police in these countries. I don't know which is more surprising—State Department "narcs" working closely with Drug Enforcement Administration (DEA) "diplomats" or joint Colombian/Peruvian military and police antidrug actions on their common border. I suspect that neither development has been given sufficient public airing.

New Alliances

The new antidrug alliances are a phenomenon almost as important in inter-American politics as the hemisphere's transition from despotism to democracy over the past 10 years. Moreover, sustaining democracy and combating the "narcoterrorist" threat are inextricably linked. That is our view, and it is the view of democratic leaders throughout the hemisphere.

How did this come about? It did not stem primarily from bureaucratic imperatives in Washington or diplomatic approaches in Lima or Bogota. And it did not result from any particular, persuasive public relations campaign. It happened, simply stated, when we discovered ourselves to be victims and began to fight back in self-defense. In effect, we began to see that the pernicious assault of drugs on society is deeply damaging to the security of our families and communities and that defending our national security has to include defending ourselves against drugs. . . .

The changes in attitude, commitment, and policy among Latin

American countries have been profound. Territorial rivalries and nationalist tensions have not disappeared, but Colombia now actively works with Peru and with Ecuador and Venezuela in interdiction. A new regional narcotics telecommunications system will soon be operating in South America. It will connect for drug law enforcement purposes military and national police establishments which not long ago saw each other as potential enemies.

Successful aerial spraying of marijuana in Mexico, Panama, Belize, and Colombia has been followed by important experiments in aerial eradication of coca by the Colombian national police. Colombia has extradited seven individuals, five of its own citizens, all accused of narcotics trafficking, to the United States. The international movement of chemicals used in the cocaine refining process has been severely restricted.

General awareness of the benefits of international cooperation to combat narcotics production and trafficking is increasing. . . . Many European countries are beginning to look into assisting eradication efforts in Latin America, as they realize that they, too, are targets of the traffickers.

Hope of Cooperation

Although drug-related corruption is pervasive in the United States, in Latin America it is eating away at the fabric of fragile democracies.

In this community of tragedy lies the hope of real cooperation between the two halves of the hemisphere. In the past, north and south were each tempted to think the problem lay in the other's backyard.

Latin Americans now understand that drugs are their problem, too. They know that the crime and corruption that accompany drugs make them a threat not just to individual residents but to the national sovereignty as well.

Gregory F. Treverton and Elliot L. Richardson, *The New York Times*, January 24, 1987.

Developments in the United States are running a parallel course. The mythology of cocaine as relatively safe, the only risk being arrest, has been exploded. Concerned Congressmen, like New York Representative [Charles] Rangel, Chairman of the House Select Committee on Narcotics Abuse and Control, have led a determined and dedicated effort to educate all of us to the dangers of drug abuse and the necessity for international cooperation. First Lady Nancy Reagan has pitched in to help carry the message to the youth of this country. Americans are coming, if slowly, to realize that cocaine does lead to addiction: after five or so uses the odds shift heavily in that direction. The corruptive potential of drug trafficking is increasingly recognized as something more than prime time script material. And basuco, the deadly partially refined coca from South America, has begun to appear in the United States along with "crack," a more refined, but nearly as deadly, form of the drug.

Collaboration

American antinarcotics activity, both domestic and foreign, has increased rapidly. Perceived sometime rivals like DEA and Customs are collaborating as never before. Similarly, the extradition of accused drug traffickers is not a one-way transit to the United-States—we have extradited two American citizens to Colombia as part of this effort. . . .

A new function has been added to the traditional tasks of Foreign Service officers. Five of our posts in Latin America and the Caribbean have something called narcotics assistance units charged with administering important programs of assistance and cooperation in the countries where they operate. These "narcodiplomats" are on the sharp edge of this critical warfare. They have been partly responsible for encouraging and helping to channel U.S. funds into the successes of Latin American governments I noted earlier. Some of them seem to be doing better in their liaison with difficult-to-deal-with ranking government officials than are their political and economic section counterparts.

One of my personal contributions to the war against illegal drugs will be to make sure that good "narcodiplomats" move up faster in the Foreign Service. The drug mafia and their guerrilla friends are shooting at these people. Few things that the State Department does contribute so directly to the U.S. national security and welfare than our coordinated war on the narcotics/terrorist combine.

The Continuing Threat

At the same time, we must be honest with ourselves. What we and many governments in the hemisphere are now doing is significant, but it does not mean that drug trafficking is being defeated. In fact, in the aggregate, we have not reduced the flow of cocaine to the United States at all. The price of the drug has gone down over the past few years in major American cities, indicating increased movement of supplies.

Enormous profits are creating sharp incentives for increases in coca acreage and for innovative production, smuggling, and marketing. The pattern of expanding cultivation is clear as one flies over the vast eastern slope of the Andes. Illicit plantings are shifted as eradication programs succeed. As Colombian interdiction, eradication, and extradition increases, the traffickers move their operations to neighboring countries. The traffickers constantly experiment with new chemistry and new smuggling routes. As our and other naval forces interdict drugs in the Caribbean, the traffic flows elsewhere. Cocaine increasingly is being transported through Mexico and across our land border. As old methods of hiding the white powder are unearthed by Customs, new, more sophisticated ways are developed. A cocaine shipment from Colombia arrived in a case of realistic plastic imitations of the ubiquitous yam.

Toward Common Goals

Narcotics trafficking is a clear and present danger. The change is that these other nations now realize that the danger is universal, that they too stand in harm's way. With that realization, we are finally beginning to work together as an international community progressing toward common goals.

Ann B. Wrobleski, *Department of State Bulletin*, August 1986.

Where does that place all of the increased cooperative efforts I have just described? It means that more, much more has to be done. But, at the very least, it also means that very few of the principal actors are now attempting to hide their own inaction by pointing the finger at others. Almost everyone is now in the act together. The experts in our agencies and in other countries are agreeing that interdiction, or eradication, or extradition, or the reduction of demand cannot work if attempted in isolation, one tactic at a time.

The problem is huge; it must be addressed across the board. The resources arrayed against our efforts are staggering. Cocaine is at least a $40-billion-dollar-a-year business. For obvious reasons, exact figures are elusive—it may be twice that. What is clear, is that everyone is affected, everyone is to blame, and everyone is responsible for action. . . .

Additional Help

Corruption and intimidation remain major problems. But, at the very least, most of these governments have stopped insisting that it is our problem and have begun to try to do something about this universal scourge. I believe they deserve more help from us and more private action on our own soil.

What kind of additional help do I think we should provide? One area which deserves to be considered is a major increase in the tools many of these countries require for drug enforcement and interdiction. I am not talking about jet fighters or aircraft carriers; but I am talking about more armored helicopters and troop-carrying aircraft. Why? Because when the police or special military units go after jungle labs today, they are likely to run into assault rifles and machine guns, not Saturday night specials. Better targeted U.S. assistance would serve U.S. national security, and it would, at the same time, demonstrate that we are listening to what the new, democratic leaders of Latin America are saying—with increasing frequency—about their real national security needs: less for military competition with their neighbors and more for defense against the trafficking and terrorizing enemy within.

Would this mean spending more? I'm not sure. American tax-payers now shell out over $1.5 billion a year, more or less evenly divided between enforcement on the one hand and treatment, prevention, and rehabilitation on the other. And of that amount, less than a $100 million is spent abroad. . . . Certainly, we could do more, much more, to stop the stuff before it reaches our shores. . . .

Time To Do More

I believe that recent history does justify more from us, both as a government and as a people. The statistics and the experiences of what drug abuse is doing to a generation and more of Americans (and Brazilians, Colombians, and Jamaicans) demands that we do more and that we end whatever indifference remains. Attacking the traffic in narcotics is as high a priority as we have in the U.S. Government. I have told my diplomats that, and the Navy is showing it by supporting the Coast Guard's mission.

Now it's the turn of the Council on Foreign Relations and of people like you. It is time to go beyond sitting in judgment on what bureaucrats and foreigners are doing. It is time to join the war against drugs. As Ecuador's president said, in somewhat more colorful terms, during a visit to a coca field to observe eradication: "Let's get rid of this garbage."

This is not just a health problem, not just a foreign aid problem, not just a police problem. It is a moral challenge and a national security matter. It threatens democracy in our hemisphere and children in our homes. Let us treat it with the seriousness it deserves.

"The international campaign . . . to eliminate illicit drugs is rapidly draining any reservoir of goodwill that may exist for the U.S. in the Third World."

Narcotics Control Has Harmed Foreign Relations

Ted Galen Carpenter

Ted Galen Carpenter is a foreign policy analyst with the Cato Institute, a conservative think tank in Washington, DC. In the following viewpoint, he says that US demands for foreign cooperation on narcotics control are straining relationships with other countries. According to Carpenter, Washington's assault on foreign drug trafficking is ineffective and is ruining US foreign relations.

As you read, consider the following questions:

1. What evidence does the author give that the US campaign against international drug trafficking has angered foreign governments?
2. According to Carpenter, what problems has the anti-narcotics campaign encountered?
3. Why does the author call the anti-drug campaign an "emotional catharsis"?

Pres. Reagan launched a new and decidedly militant phase in the U.S. campaign to halt global narcotics trafficking when he sent American troops to Bolivia. The secrecy of this drug eradication operation (code named Blast Furnace) vanished even before the first helicopters arrived, and the Bolivian people soon witnessed a "media event" with more than a few comic-opera overtones. Dozens of U.S. military and Drug Enforcement Administration (DEA) personnel, along with Bolivian forces, pursued cocaine smugglers through the countryside with scant success. Despite massive preparation, the raids uncovered only two drug labs (out of an estimated 80-100 in the region) and failed to net a single major trafficker.

In several respects, the Bolivian episode is symbolic of the Reagan Administration's campaign against the international narcotics trade. It was ill-conceived, clumsy, and futile. The sight of U.S. troops conducting quasi-military missions in a small Latin American nation is almost certain to revive the specter of "Yankee imperialism" throughout the hemisphere. Yet, Administration leaders seem oblivious to the foreign policy risks they are incurring.

The basic features of the Reagan Administration's "war on drugs" began to emerge as early as September, 1981, when the President addressed the annual meeting of the International Association of Chiefs of Police. Mapping a comprehensive assault on the drug problem, he not only expressed a desire to strengthen domestic law enforcement and educational efforts to stem consumer demand, but also stressed the need to discourage international production and distribution. His proposed "narcotics enforcement strategy" included "a foreign policy that vigorously seeks to interdict and eradicate illicit drugs, wherever cultivated, processed, or transported.". . .

A Vigorous War

Since Reagan's speech, various Federal agencies, including the State Department, the Drug Enforcement Administration (DEA), and the Central Intelligence Agency, have waged a vigorous war to eliminate narcotics production and distribution around the globe. The U.S. government has enticed or coerced numerous foreign governments into adopting programs to eradicate drug crops and to intercept narcotics shipments passing through their jurisdictions. U.S. officials urge growers to substitute other crops for the production of illicit varieties and offer them compensation during the transition. Congress and the Administration channel millions of dollars into training and equipping foreign anti-narcotics law-enforcement agencies.

Despite much rhetorical bravado and a few highly publicized successes, the U.S. effort has been a bitter disappointment. There has been virtually no reduction in the aggregate amount of cocaine, heroin, and marijuana coming into the U.S. This failure has created an impetus to search for scapegoats. Anti-drug militants in Congress, such as Sens. Paula Hawkins (R.-Fla.), Jeremiah Denton (R.-Ala.), and Strom Thurmond (R.-S. Car.), charge that some foreign governments exhibit insufficient zeal in ferreting out narcotics traffickers. They threaten to propose legislation imposing trade sanctions and other penalties against recalcitrant regimes. Congressional conservatives and their ideological brethren in the Administration also increasingly identify the narcotics issue with the larger Cold War. They assert that Cuba, Bulgaria, Nicaragua, and other Marxist states are trafficking in drugs as part of a conspiracy to "destabilize" American society.

International Embarrassment

The principal focus of the Reagan Administration's "supply-side" campaign against drugs has been on interdicting shipments from abroad and pressuring foreign governments to get tough with domestic producers.

As it has become evident that this rather expensive effort has had marginal success at best, finger-pointing at other societies has accelerated. The practice has complicated our relations with a strategically vital and increasingly vulnerable region. Occasionally it has resulted in profound embarrassment.

Jody Powell, *Los Angeles Times*, June 1, 1986.

Even more disturbing than the heightened temper of domestic rhetoric is the evidence of adverse foreign policy ramifications. Regimes normally friendly to the U.S. are annoyed at America's anti-drug obsession, especially the insensitive (on occasion, even boorish) behavior of the Reagan Administration toward foreign governments not sharing the same attitude. Drug-crop eradication and substitution programs antagonize peasants and other growers, creating a reservoir of ill will toward the U.S. and toward governments that seem subservient to U.S. dictates. Throughout Asia and Latin America, the U.S. drug agent is rapidly becoming the new "ugly American." Washington's international anti-narcotics crusade is an operational failure that threatens to become a diplomatic catastrophe. . . .

Indifference and Opposition

America's international anti-narcotics campaign has confronted numerous problems. Despite considerable propaganda to the contrary, U.S. officials encounter indifference and sometimes outright opposition from foreign leaders. Even worse, evidence demonstrates that high-level foreign officials are themselves often involved in narcotics trafficking or at least countenance it. This official corruption, combined with an increasing willingness on the part of narcotics czars to employ violence to defend their operations, has thrown Washington's anti-drug offensive into disarray.

U.S. leaders concede that they have struggled to overcome a pervasive assumption on the part of Third World governments that narcotics trafficking is an "American problem." Foreign officials have responded to U.S. anti-drug programs with apathy and resentment. Bolivian Undersecretary of the Interior Gustavo Sanchez epitomized the latter attitude when he asserted that he and his countrymen were putting their lives in danger "to prevent drugs from entering the U.S." A Panamanian official was even more caustic. "The U.S. is to blame for most of this mess," he fumed. "If there weren't the frightening demand in the States, we wouldn't even have to worry about trying to eliminate the supply."

Several reasons account for this dissatisfaction. Until recently, most drug-producing nations did not have serious internal drug-abuse problems; consequently, they saw the U.S. sense of urgency as either overwrought or self-serving. Third World leaders concluded that they were being asked to assume an onerous law enforcement burden merely to alleviate an American problem. To overcome this attitude, Washington resorted to a combination of economic inducements and threatened sanctions.

Strengthening the perception of narcotics abuse as merely an American problem is a significant cultural difference; many, although assuredly not all, Asian and Latin American societies exhibit a more permissive attitude toward moderate drug use. Opium has long enjoyed a quasi-legitimate status in Southeast Asia, for example. Similarly, the Andean societies of Colombia, Ecuador, Peru, and Bolivia employ raw coca and the coca plant itself for a variety of accepted uses. Rural Jamaicans often drink tea brewed from marijuana for medicinal purposes. This cultural difference accounts for much of the apathy of other governments toward U.S. drug-eradication and interdiction programs. . . .

Draining Goodwill

The international campaign of the U.S. government to eliminate illicit drugs is rapidly draining any reservoir of goodwill that may exist for the U.S. in the Third World. By encouraging friendly regimes to destroy profitable crops grown by heretofore impoverished peasants, Washington inadvertently undermines popular support for those often-fragile governments, and leftist guerrillas are quick to seize the opportunity. The Administration antagonizes other foreign governments by using a crude carrot-and-stick approach to secure their cooperation in the global war

THE BEST AND THE WITTIEST by Gary Brookins. © 1986, Richmond Times Dispatch. Dist. by News America Syndicate, 1986 by permission of North America Syndicate, Inc.

on drugs, even though they might not share the same sense of urgency. Just as Third World peoples resist being drawn into Cold War struggles between the Soviet Union and the U.S., they bitterly resent being dragooned into campaigns designed to solve what they see as essentially an American domestic problem. Their resentment is justified.

U.S. policymakers must face the reality that American drug abuse is primarily an internal matter and that the solution (if any) can be found only within the borders of the U.S. It is a basic economic principle that, as long as demand for a product exists, suppliers will attempt to satisfy that demand—only the price will vary. Because the domestic demand for marijuana, cocaine, and other illicit drugs remains high, it is inevitable that both domestic and foreign producers will continue to operate. This is particularly true in view of the fact that anti-drug laws create a risk factor that artificially inflates the retail price of narcotics. One may well argue that the most effective way to decrease drug imports would be to legalize consumption. The resulting lower prices would squeeze profit margins, thereby discouraging foreign traffickers. This alternative at least merits consideration, given that the existing approach is clearly not working.

The Reagan Administration's campaign to interdict the supply of drugs is little more than a collective emotional catharsis, a desperate attempt to compensate for previous and current failures to stem domestic demand. It is an inherently futile gesture. Even in the unlikely event that Washington does succeed in significantly reducing the global narcotics supply, the domestic drug problem would not thereby be alleviated. U.S. officials acknowledge that crops of marijuana, opium poppies, and coca leaves exceed current demand by a considerable margin. Thus, even successful eradication efforts would merely reduce an existing surplus. At most, such a "victory" might temporarily increase the price of drugs to the consumer, but it would achieve no lasting impact on consumption.

Above all, both the people and the government of the U.S. must recognize that drug use in this country is a *domestic* concern. Attempting to find in other nations the solution to our problem is futile and counterproductive; it merely provokes resentment on the part of foreign populations, antagonizes or undermines otherwise friendly governments, and seriously complicates—and compromises—U.S. foreign policy. Washington's international anti-drug campaign is an ill-conceived, irredeemable failure that should be abolished as soon as possible.

a critical thinking activity

Distinguishing Primary from Secondary Sources

A critical thinker must always question his or her source of knowledge. One way to critically evaluate information is to be able to distinguish between *primary sources* (a "firsthand" or eyewitness account from personal letters, documents, or speeches, etc.) and *secondary sources* (a "secondhand" account usually based upon a "firsthand" account and possibly appearing in newspapers, encyclopedias, or other similar types of publications). A diary about the Civil War written by a Civil War veteran is an example of a primary source. A history of the Civil War written many years after the war and relying, in part, upon that diary for information is an example of a secondary source.

However, it must be noted that interpretation and/or point of view also play a role when dealing with primary and secondary sources. For example, the historian writing about the Civil War not only will quote from the veteran's diary but also will interpret it. It is certainly a possibility that his or her interpretation may be incorrect. Even the diary or primary source must be questioned as to interpretation and point of view. The veteran may have been a militarist who stressed the glory of warfare rather than the human suffering involved.

This activity is designed to test your skill in evaluating sources of information. Pretend that you are writing a research paper on drug abuse. You decide to include an equal number of primary and secondary sources. Listed below are a number of sources which may be useful in your research. Carefully evaluate each of them. First, place a *P* next to those descriptions you feel would serve as primary sources. Second, rank the primary sources assigning the number (1) to the most objective and accurate primary source, number (2) to the next accurate and so on until the ranking is finished. Repeat the entire procedure, this time placing an *S* next to those descriptions you feel would serve as secondary sources and then ranking them.

If you are doing this activity as a member of a class or group, discuss and compare your evaluation with other members of the group. If you are reading this book alone, you may want to ask others if they agree with your evaluation. Either way, you will find the interaction very valuable.

1. An estimate by the Customs Service of the amount of drugs entering the US every year.

2. A magazine interview with the President of Colombia outlining the country's drug-eradication program.

3. A historical study of the US Drug Enforcement Agency and its international policies.

4. A documentary of Latin American farmers on small farms struggling with new crops after eradication of their cocaine crops.

5. Viewpoint three from this chapter.

6. A biography of a wealthy and powerful drug trafficker from the 1920s.

7. The eyewitness account by a US Customs officer following a major Florida drug bust.

8. An editorial about the need for more federal funds to stop drug trafficking across the US-Mexican border.

9. A chapter on the drug trade in a book about Latin America and US foreign policy.

10. A televised confession of a former pusher linking the mafia and foreign drug operations.

11. A letter addressed to the US secretary of state from the president of Bolivia, asking for US aid to help destroy Bolivian narcotics crops.

12. An interview with a Pakistani drug trafficker extradited to the US to face drug charges.

13. A novel describing the experiences of a drug enforcement agent along the US-Mexico border.

14. A letter to the editor of a daily newspaper criticizing US treatment of a notorious drug trafficker.

15. A newspaper report of drug prices in three major US cities since the implementation of foreign drug policies.

Periodical Bibliography

The following articles have been selected to supplement the diverse views expressed in this chapter.

Angus Deming — "Guns, Drugs, and Politics," *Newsweek*, July 28, 1986.

Mathea Falco — "The Big Business of Illicit Drugs," *The New York Times Magazine*, December 11, 1983.

Edward I. Koch — "An Arsenal for the Federal War on Drugs," *The New York Times*, July 18, 1986.

Flora Lewis — "Tall Is Not High," *The New York Times*, March 22, 1985.

Susanna McBee — "Flood of Drugs—A Losing Battle," *U.S. News & World Report*, March 25, 1985.

James Mills — "The Simplest Way To Fight Drugs," *The New York Times*, September 5, 1986.

Charles B. Rangel — "Drug Traffic Can—And Must—Be Curbed," *USA Today*, May 1984.

John Russonello and Nancy Belden — "Colombians Deal with Drugs," *Public Opinion*, September/October 1986.

William Safire — "Issue: Posse Comitatus," *The New York Times*, February 28, 1986.

Lewis A. Tambs — "A War that Must Be Won: Drugs and South America," *Vital Speeches of the Day*, August 15, 1985.

Clyde D. Taylor — "Links Between International Narcotics Trafficking and Terrorism," *Department of State Bulletin*, August 1985.

Jon R. Thomas — "International Campaign Against Drug Trafficking," *Department of State Bulletin*, January 1985.

Mary Thornton — "'Mexico Vice' Is Too Much for Customs," *The Washington Post National Weekly Edition*, May 12, 1986.

R. Dean Tice — "Fighting the Drug Flow," *Defense*, May/June 1986.

Gregory F. Treverton and Elliot L. Richardson — "A Three-Front War on Drugs," *The New York Times*, January 24, 1987.

Should Drug Testing Be Used?

DRUG ABUSE

Chapter Preface

Drug abuse is a problem that cuts across all demographic boundaries. Many adults have only read about it in the paper or worried about it when their children went to school, but now more of them are feeling the impact of the crackdown on drug abuse in their workplaces: Those who have never personally used illegal drugs are being asked by their employers to submit to drug tests. Suddenly the abstract problem becomes personal, and questions over the testing's usefulness, legality, and accuracy arise. The debate centers on the desire to stop drug abuse versus the need to protect individual liberties.

Drug testing, many employers and employees will testify, can be an extremely effective way to curb drug abuse in the workplace. The US military began testing for drugs in 1982 and claims to have cut drug abuse by half among military personnel. When President and Mrs. Reagan announced the War on Drugs in 1986, they encouraged executives to implement drug testing in their companies. Many of those who have done so have reported improved employee performance and reduced absenteeism.

These benefits, however, do not eliminate the worry that drug testing may violate civil rights. Many people are deeply concerned that urinalysis constitutes an invasion of privacy. They are afraid that this breach of individual rights will lead to more serious violations such as mandatory polygraph tests or computers that spy on employees.

No one wants to risk losing the rights Americans have worked so hard to maintain. Yet many segments of the work force remain plagued by illegal narcotics. The task that lies ahead is to protect workers' rights and still keep a check on drug abuse. Finding a suitable compromise will continue to be one of the challenges in the fight against drugs.

"Asking people to produce a urine specimen ... is an unwarranted invasion of their privacy."

Drug Testing Violates Workers' Rights

The New Republic

Of all the issues in the debate over drug testing, individual rights is perhaps the most controversial. In the following viewpoint, the editors of *The New Republic* magazine object to random urinalysis on the grounds that it violates the right to privacy. Random testing of the American work force, they write, is unconstitutional and unnecessary and could lead to even greater rights violations.

As you read, consider the following questions:

1. What statistics do the editors cite to show the widespread use of drug testing?
2. Under what circumstances might drug testing be justified, according to the authors?
3. According to the authors, why do drug tests and similar invasions of privacy appeal so strongly to those who run businesses?

The New Republic, "The Yellow Peril," March 31, 1986. Reprinted by permission of THE NEW REPUBLIC, © 1986, The New Republic, Inc.

The President's Commission on Organized Crime spent 32 months and nearly five million dollars preparing its report on drug abuse and trafficking. There's something for everyone in the panel's 1,000-page study, but here's the gist of its recommendation: since law-enforcement techniques have failed to curtail the supply of illegal narcotics, we should try to diminish the demand. In pursuit of that goal, the commission argues, the president should direct all federal agencies to implement "suitable drug testing programs." State and local governments and the private sector should follow suit, and federal contracts should be denied to firms that don't test for drugs. In other words, practically everyone should have his or her urine tested. Laboratory owners and manufacturers of small plastic cups should be delighted with the scheme.

Several members of the panel have dissented publicly, saying that the controversial suggestion was added without their knowledge. U.S. Court of Appeals Judge Irving R. Kaufman, who chairs the commission and supports the idea, has refused to answer their objections. But the report has been greeted with signs of approbation as well. Attorney General Edwin Meese III caused some confusion in the press when he stopped short of endorsing the plan (saying it might be too expensive), yet argued that drug testing doesn't violate anyone's constitutional rights. Representative Clay Shaw of Florida embraced the idea unreservedly. He volunteered himself and his staff for urine tests as soon as they can be arranged.

Too Close for Comfort

In fact, we are already much closer to universal urine testing than most people realize. One-quarter of all Fortune 500 companies, including IBM and General Motors, now administer urinalysis tests to applicants or current employees. Another 20 percent are planning to institute programs. . . . According to a *USA Today* survey cited in the Kaufman Commission report, two-thirds of those firms won't hire anyone who fails a test. Of those testing current employees, 25 percent fire those who fail, while 64 percent require treatment, strongly recommend it, or take disciplinary action. Since a urine sample is usually taken as part of a medical examination, applicants and employees often don't know that they are being checked for drug use.

The tests are probably justified for air traffic controllers and Drug Enforcement Administration agents who now undergo them regularly. There's even a case to be made for testing professional athletes, part of whose job is to serve as role models to children. But need the same standards be applied to the entire work force? The *Los Angeles Times*, the *Chicago Tribune*, and the *New York Times*, for example, screen all new employees for drug use.

Although the *New York Times* doesn't tell applicants that their urine will be tested for narcotics, a spokesman says the company's policy is to not hire anyone whose medical examination indicates use of illegal drugs, including marijuana. Once you are hired, there are no further tests.

And urinalysis is only one of the more intrusive new ways to search people for drugs. Many bus drivers and amusement-park ride operators are required to produce saliva samples, which are tested for the presence of marijuana. . . . It is now possible to test hair samples for drugs. Some companies have searched lockers

Guardiangraphic by Van Howell. Reprinted with permission.

and cars, frisked workers on their way into the factory, and set up hidden video cameras. G.M. hired undercover agents to pose as assembly-line workers in order to catch drug dealers. Capital Cities/ABC and the *Kansas City Times and Star* called off the drug-sniffing dogs after reporters ridiculed their plans for canine searches in the newsroom.

There is already a body of case law on the Fourth Amendment questions raised by the various drug tests. If a warrant is required to search someone's home, you need a probable cause to impound some of his urine. The Kaufman report notes that the Supreme Court ruled in favor of the Federal Railroad Administration's right to employ a range of tests for drugs and alcohol. But the commission ignores that fact that the railroad regulations delineate the need for "reasonable suspicion" that employees are under the influence on the job—not that they've used drugs away from work in previous weeks.

Invasion of Privacy

Beyond the constitutional questions, most would agree that asking people to produce a urine specimen if they want to apply for a job, or to keep the one they've got, is an unwarranted invasion of their privacy. To assure an honest sample, a supervisor must witness its production. The Coast Guard has someone follow each of its 38,000 employees into the bathroom. "We don't want them to bring in baby's urine," one Coast Guard officer told the *Washington Post*.

Why are these officers and supervisors, who administer the tests, always assumed to be clean? Programs for widespread testing almost always reflect class bias. Regulations are usually written for equipment operators or assembly-line workers without reference to supervisors or management. Isn't it just as important that they be drug-free? If we test train conductors, shouldn't we also analyze the urine of the railroad bosses? As the Kaufman Commission report indicates, heroin has been climbing up the socioeconomic ladder as cocaine has been descending. Yet lawyers, stock brokers, and senators are rarely included in drug-testing programs, perhaps because they are better able to fight the imposition of such indignities.

Besides running roughshod over personal privacy, the tests are impractical and imprecise. Urinalysis can't tell you whether someone is high on the job—only whether she has traces of narcotics in her system. Cocaine, heroin, and PCP—the drugs employers claim to be most worried about—vanish from the bloodstream in less than 48 hours. If the tests are scheduled, as most are, an employee can avoid detection by staying clean for a couple of days.

But THC, the active chemical in marijuana, remains in the blood months after it is ingested. That's why the vast majority of those who fail drug tests register positive for pot. What do we do with them? Nearly 40 million citizens smoke marijuana at least once a year. Half that number use the drug regularly. Should all of them be fired? If passing a drug test ought to be a condition of all kinds of employment, should a large segment of the population be unemployable? Eleven states have eliminated criminal penalties for possession of marijuana, and Alaskans can grow it legally in their backyards. Rather than weeding 20 million weed-smokers from the work force, employers ought to discipline, treat, or fire those who perform poorly at work, whether or not they use drugs. Axing workers who test positive but demonstrate no other problems doesn't make sense.

Unconstitutional

Even if drug tests were free and 100 percent accurate, they would still be unconstitutional. There is going to be a lot of legal rhubarb over this, and I don't know what a Rehnquist-led Supreme Court is finally going to decide. But I take the same attitude toward the Constitution as Reformation Protestants took toward the Bible: Anyone can read it and witness the truth thereof. Amendment Four is perfectly straightforward:

> The right of the people to be secure in their persons, houses, papers and effects against unreasonable searches and seizures shall not be violated, and no warrants shall issue but upon probable cause, supported by an oath or affirmation and particularly describing the place to be searched and the persons or things to be seized.

It's hard to see how scatter-shot drug testing could be legal under the Fourth Amendment, no matter how particularly the Government describes the way you take a leak.

P.J. O'Rourke, *Playboy*, February 1987.

Like those who advocate widespread use of polygraph tests, the Kaufman panel puts boundless faith in far-from-perfect scientific techniques. Although the tests have been widely used for only a few years, they've ruined lives and fingered thousands of innocent people. The Pentagon, which administers six million urinalysis tests a year, provides plenty of examples. Urinalysis tests said time and again that a Navy doctor named Dale Mitchell was using morphine. When he failed a polygraph test, he began sending out job applications. Then someone at the Navy lab figured out that Mitchell was testing positive for poppy seed bagels. In 1982 and 1983 a group of 9,100 employees the Army said were using illegal drugs weren't so lucky. They had already gotten their dishonorable discharges when the Pentagon tried to track them down to apologize for convicting them on faulty evidence including mixed-up samples.

Most drug-testing laboratories acknowledge a margin of error of two or three percent. Even by that conservative estimate, four million innocents would lose their jobs if we tested the entire work force. But the conclusions of a secret study of the labs by the National Centers for Disease Control are far less optimistic. According to an article in the *Journal of the American Medical Association*, the worst laboratories indicated false positive results as much as 66 percent of the time. Only one lab was credited with acceptable performance in testing for cocaine. The CDC study didn't include any marijuana samples, which pose similar, if not more severe, lab problems. Herbal tea and prescription drugs can trigger false positive results, as can being in a room with people smoking marijuana. Those terminated unfairly may waste years and fortunes proving their innocence, if they are able to do so at all.

Little Plastic Cups

Despite the abundant hype, the use of legal and illegal drugs has decreased markedly over the past several years. Fewer people are taking heroin, PCP, marijuana, alcohol, and tobacco than they were ten years ago. LSD and Quaaludes have all but vanished. Cocaine use has increased slightly, but may well decline when its dangers become better known—which is what happened with heroin and PCP.

The failure of our policy of interdiction has combined with the hysteria to send the law-enforcement establishment on a search for sweeping solutions. [Attorney General Edwin] Meese suggested stepping up efforts to prosecute consumers of illegal drugs. What sort of indiscriminate check will catch the corporate imagination next? Strip searches for weapons? Polygraphs for potential office thieves? Blood tests for AIDS? All hold forth a similar promise of purity in the workplace, which is why they appeal so strongly to those who run businesses and governments. But such forms of social control, which force people to provide their innocence of crimes they haven't even been charged with, are abhorrent. What starts with little plastic cups ends in the urinalysis state.

"Drug testing may well be our last line of defense."

Drug Testing Does Not Violate Workers' Rights

Courtland Milloy and Jesse Philips

Courtland Milloy is a columnist for *The Washington Post*. Jesse Philips is the founder and chairman of Philips Industries Inc. in Dayton, Ohio. In the following viewpoint, both stress the need for drug testing in spite of claims that it violates workers' rights. In Part I, Milloy describes the urgent nature of the drug epidemic and contends that the harm inflicted by abusers justifies testing. In Part II, Philips outlines employers' responsibilities to stop drug abuse in the workplace. Drug testing, he says, is a necessary first step toward such a goal.

As you read, consider the following questions:

1. What examples does Milloy give to show that drug abuse is serious enough to justify testing?
2. According to Milloy, why is testing the only way to reach drug addicts?
3. How will drug testing help clean up the workplace, according to Philips?

I

A person I know said he had smoked marijuana for more than 10 years when he heard that his employer, the Air Force Reserves, was about to start a drug testing program. Until then, he thought he was hooked on the stuff, but the prospects of losing his job made him stop—cold turkey. This is the kind of testimonial we'll probably be hearing a lot about as the controversy over drug testing in the work place comes to a head in courts across the country. Already, there is a dramatic reduction in drug use among college athletes who are subject to testing, and the same appears to be true among military personnel.

Why, then, are so many people opposed to drug testing?

In a case involving the U.S. Customs Service, employees contend that testing is a violation of their civil rights. A federal court has ruled in their favor, saying that probable cause for suspicion of drug use must be shown before a person can be ordered to submit to a test.

Under ordinary circumstances, if drugs were not undermining the fabric of this country, corrupting law enforcement and politicians alike, this would be an acceptable excuse. But for U.S. Customs Service employees, of all people, to refuse such tests does little to instill confidence in a group that is critical to our effort to stop the flow of drugs into this country.

Our Last Defense

I am obviously no lawyer, and my civil liberties card will no doubt be revoked but all one needs to do is walk the streets of this country—from Wall Street to the back streets—to know that drastic action is called for in the war on drugs, and that drug testing may well be our last line of defense.

Although we hear about the availability of drugs in our community, I believe people would be outraged if they knew how many school-aged children were starting out on what may well become a lifelong dependency on drugs. There is only one way to reach them. It is not telling them to "say no to drugs." It is to test them, and the deterrent effect alone would be worth the fuss.

Before this day is over, more than 1,000 people will dial a toll-free cocaine hot line. Most of them will be relatively well-off people, half of them women. When people pick up a phone in an effort to save their own life, you know they have a serious problem. But the greater problem is that more than 20 million people use illegal drugs regularly and instead of calling for help they are driving cars, flying airplanes, sailing boats and operating all manner of hazardous equipment.

There is obviously only one way to reach them, and testing—for all its faults and imprecision—is the only way. Indeed the necessary technical improvements and testing methods can be made.

What must be faced here is that we are dealing with a spoiled baby boom generation that is having serious problems coping with the pain of growing up. There is no other explanation for America to be in the midst of a drug epidemic unlike anywhere else in the world. These people need help, even though they don't know how to ask for it—in fact, would not ask for it anymore than they would have asked for a dose of castor oil as children.

Despite the ravaging effects of drug use today, the situation will likely get worse in the near future.

The case of the naval laboratory chemist who was caught mixing up a batch of synthetic heroin 1,000 times more potent than pure China white is a harbinger of what is being cooked up in the drug world's next assault on our sensibilities. There is now synthetic cocaine more powerful than anything that has been on the market to date, and more PCP than ever with recipes so simple that kids can cook it up at home.

Not Too Much To Ask

Just as a law drafting men for military service may be justified even though it "reduces the personal freedom of every American" subject to the law, so also may drug testing be proper if its objective is of sufficient importance. And it follows as a corollary that what might not be desirable under one set of circumstances might become appropriate under different circumstances.

There is a general consensus that the drug problem is rapidly attaining a magnitude that threatens our national well-being. It may not be too much to ask every American, including those who do not use drugs, that he or she submit to a reduction of personal freedom if doing so may contribute to the elimination of this cancer in our society.

Julian H. Brachfeld, *The New York Times*, September 1, 1986.

There are already too many addicts in our society, with thousands—perhaps millions—more in the making. As robbers, burglars, murderers and generally just sick people on the loose, they are much more likely to infringe on our constitutional rights than drug testing.

II

Attorney General Edwin Meese III spoke out on the responsibility of management to curb drug abuse in the workplace. His message was obscured by an outcry against what ACLU Director Ira Glasser referred to as "a totalitarian kind of response which will injure tens of millions of innocent people in an attempt to find the few who are using drugs and alcohol."

While the theorists contemplate the ethics and legality of management efforts in this regard, real managers must cope with a problem that, according to Mr. Meese's figures, costs employers $7,000 for each drug-abusing employee. Responsible managers recognize that a relatively drug-free, dignified workplace is not the responsibility of government; the buck stops at management's desk. Nor is the bottom line of drug-abuse prevention a question of morals or social responsibility or increased productivity or reduced absenteeism. It's merely a question of good old-fashioned business management.

Concern About Drug Abuse

And as I found out after writing a letter of inquiry to each of our workers at their home address, managers are not the only ones concerned with drug abuse in the workplace. American workers may gripe or be indifferent to corporate goals, but they are generally loyal, honest, caring, hard-working individuals. They very much resent having workers around them who are using drugs, who are unreliable and who are not carrying their own load.

To quote some workers' letters: "I believe it is unfair that a person using drugs which destroy mind and body should receive the same rewards in pay and benefits I do." Another wrote, "As a single parent I have enough to worry about just putting food on my table and clothes on our backs, without worrying about drugs and alcohol." And, "With all the glass, metal and machinery in here, everyone needs to be alert and careful at all times to keep from getting hurt themselves or hurting someone else. I'll be glad to support the drug program anyway I can.". . .

I believe almost every company, large and small, has a drug-abuse problem. Philips Industries has 7,500 employees located in over 40 plants in 23 states. These are mostly small plants in rural or outlying communities. The manager of one plant wrote me that since he had a mature work force located in a rural area, he did not have a drug problem. But the workers in that same plant wrote quite the contrary: They had an acute problem.

An Acute Problem

Yet I am not ready to fault the plant manager. How was he to know? He had no experience with people using or selling drugs. He could readily spot drunken behavior. Drugs, however, are a different story. The physical effects of drug abuse are not usually as readily manifest or observable. That's why they are so insidious. In many cases we are not aware of drug use until something untoward happens.

Thus, we have begun a crash program for our managers, alerting them to warning signals indicating drug abuse—a marked increase in errors or accidents by the worker, excessive absenteeism, excessive confrontations with other workers, etc. And we are alerting our managers that once they spot these warning signals, they must avoid rash firings. This is not a witch hunt. We are trying to help our workers and our company by helping people to become productive again.

Nor can we expect Personnel to take the full load of responsibility. It is powerless to act unless it has a clearly defined policy and program. One personnel manager in a plant close to the Mexican border reported that in view of his turnover, he was not able to find drug-free, qualified personnel or to be as selective as he would like. And this problem is not limited to areas normally associated with drug use. In one of our plants in the Farm Belt, 71% of those applying for a second shift failed a drug-screening test.

The Importance of Testing

The point is that we will probably never completely eliminate drugs from the workplace. However, once the word gets around a community that your company insists on drug testing for new applicants, drug abusers are likely to think twice before applying. For those who haven't heard, we have posted large notices in our application areas alerting job-seekers that we are committed to ending drug abuse and that drug testing will be part of the application procedure. Just this small effort will turn away a number of drug abusers who could have ended up costing us too much money.

Unreasonable Searches Are Not the Issue

Opponents of random mandatory drug testing claim that it is a violation of the Fourth Amendment. They are wrong. It is not a Fourth Amendment issue. It is a public-safety issue. It is an issue of ensuring that those whose job performance directly affects the public safety are qualified to perform efficiently. It is no more intrusive than the requirement for periodic eye, heart and mental-health examinations that officers undergo routinely to ensure their fitness.

Daryl F. Gates, *Los Angeles Times*, February 13, 1987.

A well-defined anti-drug-abuse policy might encompass the following three points: 1) pre-hiring tests; 2) selective testing, where abnormal or erratic behavior suggests it's necessary; 3) a rehabilitative program. The program should be devised to protect the rights of privacy and the dignity of the vast majority of our law-abiding workers. I find nothing wrong with properly administered urine tests. Our top 27 executives, including myself, have been tested. But again, the point is not to fire everyone with a trace of drugs in his body. The idea is to help in spotting drug abusers and offering them help before they destroy themselves and hurt the company.

The solution to our drug problem calls for a hands-on approach. It cannot be approached as a line budget item with cost-benefit analysis. When we began to consider our options, a division president pointed out to me that pre-hiring tests were not in his budget. Based on his turnover, it would probably cost $60,000 and he did not see how he could offset that expense. But the intangible human costs cannot be equated in dollars.

Getting the Job Done

Business and industry do not need money to clean up our work environment—we have the funds. What we do need to get the job done is leadership. Unfortunately, all too many executives are sitting on their hands waiting for the signal to get started. True, a goodly number of companies have started pre-hiring tests— probably a good first step. Yet, the vast majority are waiting for guidelines as to what is expected and how far they should go.

Here is where we need President Reagan. We need the president to use his great leadership talents to form an alliance of business and industry to clean up the workplace. Given the proper leadership support by the president, the private sector can clean up its own house—probably without any government funding.

===

"The tests employed in screening programs have a significant error rate."

===

Drug Testing Is Unreliable

Morris J. Panner and Nicholas A. Christakis

Much of the debate on drug testing revolves around its reliability. Laboratories claim that their results are accurate while employees protest that they often are not. Morris J. Panner and Nicholas A. Christakis contend in the following viewpoint that urinalysis tests are never one hundred percent reliable and should not be used to determine employee drug abuse. Relying on drug tests should be avoided, they say, because the tests may result in false accusations. Morris J. Panner is a student at Harvard Law School. Nicholas A. Christakis is a student at Harvard Medical School.

As you read, consider the following questions:

1. Why, according to the authors, is mass drug screening "dangerously alluring"?
2. What do the authors mean by "sensitivity" and "specificity"?
3. Why is it impossible to create a completely accurate drug test, according to the authors?

Morris J. Panner and Nicholas A. Christakis, "The Limits of Science in On-The-Job Drug Screening," *The Hastings Center Report*, December 1986. Reproduced by permission. © The Hastings Center.

Screening to obtain information about medical problems such as cervical cancer or hypertension is widely used and recommended within the medical community. Increasingly, however, biomedical tests are being used in a way that reveals social and personal information. Scientific tests now offer the possibility of knowledge not only about an individual's health, but also about such things as his or her sexual, drug, or alcohol history.

The use of tests in this way is spreading. The armed services have already instituted mass screening for antibodies to the Human Immunodeficiency Virus (HIV), which causes AIDS. Screening is moving into the private sector as well; many insurance companies are testing for HIV antibodies before providing health or life insurance. Moreover, the Centers for Disease Control (CDC) recommended that counseling and voluntary testing be offered on a routine basis to all people at increased risk of being exposed to HIV.

Testing for Substance Abuse

Biomedical tests are also being used in an effort to decrease drug and alcohol abuse. Part of the effort to decrease drunk driving has involved stopping people at roadblocks and elsewhere and subjecting them to blood or breath alcohol determinations. And, as the consequences of drug abuse have become apparent, random drug testing has been established in the military, athletic, and private sectors. . . .

When used in this way, biomedical tests are transposed, to some extent, from their medical context into a realm where test results assume social, political, and legal significance. Unlike the situation in clinical medicine, stigma and possible retribution are attached to testing positively for drug abuse or HIV antibodies. Thus, legal and ethical debate has begun to focus on the proper use of these tests and of their results.

The case of screening for drug abuse illustrates some of the problems encountered when medical tests are used in a nonmedical context. Moreover, the issue of drug screening is especially pressing because the President's Commission on Organized Crime recommended that all U.S. companies test their employees for drug use. As an incentive, it urged that the federal government refuse to award contracts to companies that did not comply with this policy. In addition, the Commission recommended that the government test all of its own employees.

A Deceptively Simple Solution

Mass drug screening offers a deceptively simple solution to the problem of drug use among workers. Administering a straightforward scientific test and thus determining someone's guilt or innocence has a dangerous allure: a person who tests positively

Bob Englehart. Reprinted with permission.

for morphine use must be a morphine user, the misguided reasoning goes. Such reasoning is founded on a misunderstanding of the scientific method. In any given group of tested employees, athletes, prisoners, or soldiers, some individuals will unavoidably be falsely accused. This is not to say that the tests are grossly inaccurate; indeed, many represent highly refined bioscientific methods and are the best of which scientists are capable. However, even a very effective test is subject to error. And the existence of scientific error poses legal and ethical questions.

In discussing the effect of science on ethical choice, Robert M. Veatch notes the danger of such an excessive reliance on science. He warned that "we may become so infatuated with our technical abilities to accumulate data and tally scores that we run the risk of seriously misunderstanding the nature of the difficult decisions that must be made. We may succumb to what might be called the 'technical criteria fallacy.'"

The tests employed in screening programs have a significant error rate. The accuracy and reliability of screening tests, the extent of unavoidable error, may be understood with the help of the so-called "predictive value model." This model assesses test performance by means of two standards: sensitivity and specificity.

108

The sensitivity of a test is an index of how well it picks up true positives for a given disease or condition (such as morphine use) from a population sample. It is a measure of how well the test does what it is supposed to do—namely, identify affected individuals. Stated more precisely, sensitivity is the frequency of positive test results in people who truly have a particular disease or condition. The higher the sensitivity, the fewer the false negatives, that is, people who test negatively but actually have the condition.

The specificity of a test is an index of how well it identifies true negatives. It is the frequency of a negative test result in people without a given condition. Alternatively, specificity may be viewed as a measure of the frequency of false positives. The higher the specificity, the fewer the false positives. . . .

Predictive value theory . . . dictates that as sensitivity increases, specificity decreases, and conversely. As we design a test with fewer false positives, we will perforce have more false negatives, and vice-versa. Thus . . . it will be *impossible* to avoid creating inaccurately typed parties (either false negatives or false positives). If an employer or other tester opted for a relatively specific test, he could be more certain that a positive test did in fact indicate drug use. But other problems would arise with this approach. A high false negative rate means that the test is not identifying all drug users. In practice, therefore, screening tests tend to be relatively sensitive.

This increased level of sensitivity at the expense of specificity causes the greatest problems for the legal system. A very sensitive test, which would result in a larger number of false positive results, would lead to more false accusations.

False Positive Rates

Even the best drug screening tests have a significant false positive rate. For example, sophisticated and widely used radioimmunoassay (RIA) screening of blood for drug abuse may yield false positive rates of 43 percent for cocaine, 21 percent for opiates, 51 percent for PCP, and 42 percent for barbiturates. Another widely used and aggressively marketed urine screening methodology, "enzyme multiplied immunoassay technique" (EMIT), is also significantly unspecific and may have false positive rates estimated at 10 percent for cocaine, 5.6 percent for opiates, 5.1 percent for barbiturates, 12.5 percent for amphetamines, and 19 percent for tetrahydrocannabinol (the active ingredient in marijuana). By contrast, because of the high sensitivity of these tests, false negatives are few.

A urine drug screen can be falsely positive for many scientific reasons. Legally obtained and medically indicated drugs may cross-react in some testing protocols so that, for example, an individual taking over-the-counter codeine (in cough syrup) may test positively on EMIT-type urine screen for opiate abuse. There are many similar examples. Alternatively, false positives can arise from a variety of operator errors such as equipment contamination or sample mislabeling. Still another factor leading to false positives is the presence of endogenous substances in the urine or serum that might confound the test.

Human Error in Drug Testing

Dozens of innocent non-dopers at a time can be falsely accused of doping, any time a lab tech neglects to completely *sanitize* a machine after a positive sample runs through it; drug particles from the positive sample will contaminate the machine, causing it to give drug-positive results on the next series of samples which run through it. There are innumerable other ways these machines can be made to misfunction, and there's absolutely no way of telling when that can happen, or how often it's already happened.

High Times, October 1986.

To detect true positives, positives on screening tests should be confirmed by an alternative analytic method that relies on different physicochemical properties of the substance in question. A variety of second-level confirmatory tests can be used following RIA or EMIT screening. The better (and more expensive) second-level tests increase the confidence in the positive result, that is, increase certainty that an individual who tests positively is in fact positive. The false-positive rate for this two-stage analysis using EMIT followed by thin-layer chromatography, for example, may realistically be expected to be on the order of 2-3 percent, depending on the drug and laboratory. For EMIT followed by gas chromatography/mass spectrometry (GC/MS), at an approximate cost of fifty dollars per sample, the false positive rate may realistically be expected to be on the order of 1 percent. Unfortunately, however, as two toxicologists point out, "because of the high cost and need for specially trained operators, most laboratories either do not have or are not able to commit a GC/MS system to routine urinalysis."

Low Testing Standards

In practice, clinical labs apparently do not routinely conform even to these scientific standards, nor is it realistic to expect them to. For instance, a CDC study of marijuana testing noted that "because of the costs involved in confirmatory procedures, confirmatory tests have not always been conducted to verify presumed positive test results." Even when multi-level testing is used, blind surveys of clinical labs across the nation, conducted by the CDC, have shown a false positive rate of up to 66 percent, depending on the drug and laboratory under consideration. Human error is presumably largely responsible. There is no reason to believe that the record will improve, since it has fluctuated but not shown a consistent upward trend since 1973 after the CDC initiated blind surveying.

In sum, the problem of false positives in biomedical screening tests will not go away. Both practical expectations about laboratory function and—more important—theoretical considerations about test design dictate an inherent fallibility for urine drug tests.

"The available testing techniques are impressively accurate and effective, and they are not, as some have suggested, inherently flawed."

Drug Testing Is Reliable

John Grabowski and Louis Lasagna

John Grabowski is assistant director of the Center for the Study of Drug Development at Tufts University. Louis Lasagna is dean of the Sackler School of Graduate Biomedical Sciences and academic dean of the School of Medicine at Tufts University. In the following viewpoint, they maintain that drug tests are technically accurate and reliable. Falsely positive test results, if they occur, are caused by human error and should not be considered the fault of the tests themselves.

As you read, consider the following questions:

1. What are some basic testing techniques listed by the authors?
2. According to the authors, what are the advantages of urine testing?
3. What distinction do the authors make between the technical merit and the social merit of drug tests?

Excerpted from John Grabowski and Louis Lasagna, "Screening for Drug Use: Technical and Social Aspects," *Issues in Science and Technology*, Winter 1987. Copyright 1987, the National Academy of Sciences, 2101 Constitution Ave., Washington, DC 20418.

Drug use is an endemic human behavior. The few cultures that have lacked naturally available psychoactive substances have taken them up with a vengeance when exposed. Laboratory and clinical research has documented that the use of drugs to alter behavior has determinants in biological mechanisms operating in concert with environmental and social factors. There is much evidence that drug use results from scientifically definable behavior that can be studied, prevented, and treated.

History provides ample evidence of the use of various substances that alter behavior and of recurrent waves of concern about drug use. The major impetus for the focus on drug abuse in the United States may be the use of cocaine among all socioeconomic groups, the publicity associated with cocaine use by the wealthy and famous, concern about cocaine use by the young, and the obvious hazards associated with abuse of this chemical agent. In turn, these concerns and the diffusion of information about detection of drugs in body fluids have resulted in proposals for drug testing in many segments of society. . . .

Demonstrably Reliable

Various techniques can be used to detect the presence of drugs in body fluids or tissues. They differ in several ways, and the utility of each is related to the goals of the testing procedure. Most important, these techniques are demonstrably reliable and sensitive when implemented within their prescribed limits.

The techniques are used to detect drug use and also to examine drug blood levels in clinical pharmacology and therapeutics studies, forensic evaluations, and other analyses. Thus, their utility goes well beyond psychoactive drugs alone and indeed beyond the discipline of pharmacology.

There are basic testing techniques that can be used to examine various sample types in addition to urine, and different samples provide different advantages. For many drugs, for example, blood samples in general reflect more accurately the current pharmacological state and probable level of behavioral effect than do urine samples. Blood samples, though, require more skill and an invasive procedure in collection. Saliva samples involve a less invasive collection procedure but also reflect less clearly the current biological state with respect to most, but not all, drugs. Even hair can be used as a sample for some assays: it retains detectable drug residues for long periods. However, adequate assays and confirmations require more hair than some test subjects are willing to provide, and the technique is generally less precise than urine testing.

Urine, however, can be tampered with both before and after collection more readily than blood, hair, or saliva samples. It is not unheard of for refractory drug users to prepare for testing by drinking large quantities of liquid (thereby diluting the sample), bringing a sample to the collection which is surreptitiously substituted, or otherwise interfering with collection. Although most of the ruses can be detected or accounted for, a National Institute on Drug Abuse research monograph by Richard L. Hawks and C. Nora Chiang includes separate chapters on problems and security issues in specimen collection, assuring technical accuracy of the results, and evaluating the overall effectiveness of laboratories that conduct testing on a contract basis. Weighing all factors, urine testing provides the most reasonable way of determining the presence of drugs (although not current drug effects) for the greatest number of substances. Furthermore, the urine specimen is most readily obtained in quantities permitting replication and confirmation.

Testing Techniques

Urine testing techniques include thin layer chromatography, high performance thin layer chromatography, gas chromatography, gas chromatography-mass spectrometry, high pressure liquid chromatography, enzyme multiplied immunoassay technique, and radioimmunoassay. The fundamental characteristics of all these techniques is that by physical means (for example, color or mass) or biological means (antibody-antigen combinations), they compare the contents of a sample to a standard. When properly implemented on carefully collected samples, all these techniques have the potential for substantial accuracy and have little risk of false positives (that is, identifying a sample as containing a drug when no drug is present).

Sensitive Testing Technology

Urinalysis is now so sensitive that it can reveal traces of marijuana in nonusers who inadvertently inhale the smoke at a party, and sophisticated equipment known as GC/MS can find cocaine residue on money that was once handled by dealers. Since drug supplies are ubiquitous and the demand for them is so unstoppable, a presidential commission has suggested that these super-tests be used to help win the war on drugs.

Ronald K. Siegel, *Omni*, August 1986.

The Department of Defense has encountered and managed to overcome many quality control problems in its sample collection, testing, and result reporting during the last decade. The laboratories used by the military are vigorously evaluated. For private industry, however, the prevailing situation calls for caution. Unless government officials introduce appropriate quality controls over all testing laboratories, industry should heed the warning, "Let the buyer beware."

Urine testing techniques vary in sensitivity (ability to detect low levels of drug), specificity (ability to differentially discriminate between a particular agent and others in its class—such as amphetamine, a prescription drug, versus phenylpropanolamine, an over-the-counter diet aid), and ability to discern qualitative (type of drug) as opposed to quantitative (amount of drug) differences. The techniques also differ in whether multiple drugs can be screened concurrently or successive assays must be performed. The requisite skill of the technicians implementing the techniques differs, although greater skill is always desirable. Cost per sample can also differ substantially depending on the technical skill and the equipment and supplies required. . . .

Accurate and Effective

The available testing techniques are impressively accurate and effective, and they are not, as some have suggested, inherently flawed. Their technical merit must be distinguished from problems and errors that may arise at a number of critical points during the collection, preparation, and testing of the sample, the preparation of the materials and hardware for conducting the test, and the reporting or interpreting of the results. . . .

The potential level of reliability using any of the [testing] . . . techniques is impressive. However, as Bryan S. Finkle, a noted forensic toxicologist has observed, "In the climate where there's money to be made, inevitably there will be incompetent and inadequately staffed laboratories . . . the tests are very easy to do badly and very difficult to do well." In the face of excellent science and poor implementation of the technology, the greatest weakness and uncertainty associated with drug testing reside in the social and policy issues surrounding use of these methods.

"Mandatory testing in schools would raise teenage consciousness about drug danger and could reduce students' abuse of toxic substances."

Student Drug Tests Should Be Mandatory

Brian Noal Mittman

Many people believe that drug use among students has increased and that it is a serious enough problem to justify mandatory drug testing. In the following viewpoint, Brian Noal Mittman, a student at Dartmouth College in Hanover, New Hampshire, supports this position. He describes the drug abuse on his campus and around the country as "shocking" and lists six ways in which urinalysis could help stop it. Mittman writes frequently for publications around the country.

As you read, consider the following questions:

1. Why does Mittman recommend new and stronger drug legislation?
2. According to the author, when and how should drug tests be administered?
3. What are the six ways in which mandatory testing could reduce drug abuse, according to the author?

Brian Noal Mittman, "Teenagers Need Drug Testing," *Union Leader*, October 20, 1986. Reprinted with the author's permission.

As a recent high school graduate I've seen rampant drug use—in schools, where students take a few "hits" before entering class; at parties, from which many kids drive home completely stoned; and even at a high school prom, where cocaine usage was high. Today's younger generation is often too accepting of drugs as a part of its life, and adults are too unwilling to implement necessary anti-drug laws. With the massive drug problem that exists in our schools today, new legislation is necessary to discourage substance abuse. Cities in Texas, New York, California and Tennessee have already implemented mandatory drug testing in some of their public schools. Such a program is needed on a national scale.

A Severe Problem

Many adults who oppose mandatory drug testing in schools are completely oblivious to the severity of the problem. Students see signs of drug usage in school, with friends, and on the street far more often than their parents. In interviews conducted by USA Today, teenagers themselves were the strongest advocates of hard-line legislation to handle drug abuse. Many parents fail to realize how rampant drug addiction is. It is no longer monopolized by problem-plagued students and inner-city schools—good students and promising athletes are often victims as well. I attended an academically-oriented, highly-competitive, affluent, suburban high school. The number of students dealing and using drugs was shocking. Parents of friends on drugs feel incapable of dealing with the problem, while others choose to ignore a child's addiction. Mandatory testing in schools would raise teenage consciousness about drug danger and could reduce students' abuse of toxic substances without depending upon their parents' guidance.

Most opponents of mandatory drug testing in schools argue that such legislation is an invasion of students' privacy—the mere fact that so many teenagers do abuse drugs is sufficient evidence that they are not mature enough to handle such problems independently.

Start in Junior High

Mandatory school drug testing should be administered to students beginning at the junior high level where many drug problems start. The test should be given by an outside organization, unassociated with our public schools. Without prior warning, testing should take place for all students at a given school on Mondays, when drugs ingested from weekend partying can still be detected. Repeated testing should be administered before reporting results to parents in order to reduce uncertainties inherent in the drug test itself. This would reduce unfounded parental suspicions of frequent use if a child simply "tried" a drug for the first time before the test date, had recently kicked a drug habit, or if

117

the test result itself was inaccurate. Finally, all information should be kept confidential between parent, child and the administering agency. Results should be kept by the administering agency—not by the school—to lessen "leaks" of confidential information.

Reducing Teen Substance Abuse

Such drug testing could reduce teen substance abuse in six ways. (1) Younger, more immature students might be deterred from future drug abuse through junior high testing and heightened awareness. (2) Individuals might refrain from drugs due to embarrassment before drug testing personnel. (3) Students would fear that surprise drug testing could result in parent notification of abuse. (4) Parents notified of their children's drug problems would seek help for them. (5) Students already addicted, fearing they might be detected, might seek help on their own. (6) School administration could take action if heavy drug use over a long period of time is detected.

Defending Our Schools' Drug Tests

One of the first cries has generally been that our new drug policy is a violation of the Constitution. We've heard the First, the Fourth, Fifth, Eighth, Ninth, 10th and 14th Amendments, that we are violating the Constitution and people's rights. I feel that, as a responsible person in charge of this school district in cooperation with my board of education, we have to provide the most safe and educationally conducive atmosphere that we can for our entire student body.

When students are involved in an illegal activity, involved in substance abuse, they are not only violating their own rights, whether they realize it or not, but when they come into school under the influence, they are beginning to violate the rights of every other student and every other person in this school system. . . . Somewhere along the line the behavioral modification that is caused by that substance being in the body will interrupt and take time away from the task of education.

Alfred L. Marbaise, *The New York Times*, November 10, 1985.

State laws (required inoculations against various diseases and periodic medical checkups) have already effected health mandates for students. Today, drug abuse has become a terrible health menace in our public schools. Any attempt to reduce this growing disease should be implemented. It's time to institute drug testing for teens.

"In their zeal to root out drugs, . . . officials must pay careful attention to the constitutional rights of students."

Mandatory Drug Tests Violate Students' Rights

Thomas J. Flygare

In the following viewpoint, Thomas J. Flygare describes a case in which students of the Carlstadt-East Rutherford school system in New Jersey were required to take urinalysis tests. Many school systems have considered such policies, but these students challenged the ruling in court and won. Flygare describes the rationale behind the court's decision, agreeing that mandatory urinalysis is a violation of students' rights to privacy. Thomas J. Flygare is an attorney with the New Hampshire law firm of Sheehan, Phinney, Bass & Green.

As you read, consider the following questions:

1. According to Flygare, what was the original purpose of the medical examination recommended for the students of Carlstadt-East Rutherford?
2. What were the students' arguments against the urinalysis testing?
3. Why, according to the author, did the court rule in favor of the students?

Thomas J. Flygare, "De Jure: Courts Foil Schools' Efforts to Detect Drugs," *Phi Delta Kappan*, December 1986. © 1986, Phi Delta Kappan, Inc.

Cracking down on drug use in the schools is a major theme for many public officials these days, all the way from the President to members of local school boards. In their zeal to root out drugs, however, these officials must pay careful attention to the constitutional rights of students. . . .

In August 1985 the Carlstadt-East Rutherford (New Jersey) Regional Board of Education adopted a policy called "Comprehensive Medical Examination." This very carefully written policy, which appears to have been thoroughly reviewed by legal counsel, required all students to have physical examinations conducted by the school medical examiner. The policy stated that the purpose of the examinations was to determine whether students suffered from "any physical defects, illnesses, or communicable diseases." In addition, the policy stated:

> These complete physical examinations will help to identify any drug or alcohol use by pupils. The detection of drug and/or alcohol use will enable the Board of Education to enter the pupil into an appropriate rehabilitation program designed to help the student recognize the danger and to remedy any problem that exists.

Each student was to provide a urine sample, obtained by a "medically appropriate method." The sample was to be tested for "the levels of protein, sugar, specific gravity, blood, and the existence or non-existence of controlled, dangerous substances, non-authorized prescription drugs . . . , and alcohol."

An Unreasonable Search

A group of students brought suit in state court seeking to block the testing of urine samples for the presence of drugs. They argued, among other things, that the drug testing constituted a general search of their bodies that violated the constitutional ban against unreasonable searches and seizures under the subterfuge of a forced medical examination. The students pointed out that for the 1984-85 school year, from a student population of 520, only 28 students had asked about or had been referred to the student counselor for drug or alcohol assistance. Included in this number were some students who denied any involvement in either alcohol or drugs, as well as some who are currently drug-and alcohol-free but were receiving follow-up services.

School officials argued that the testing of the urine samples for the presence of drugs or alcohol was incidental to a number of traditional medical tests for which a urine sample is taken. Moreover, they argued, even if a student tested positive for either drugs or alcohol, no civil or criminal penalties would be imposed. In such cases, the doctor, parent, and student would discuss the problem and decide whether remedial actions were appropriate. The files maintained in accordance with the physical examination, including the drug and alcohol testing, would be kept confidential and separate from other school files. School officials emphasized their view that drug and alcohol abuse is an illness and not a criminal infraction. Therefore, they argued, the urine testing did not constitute an unreasonable search.

Drug Tests Are Disrespectful

Colleges and universities have a biting argument against forced drug testing and its prejudgments. An undergraduate college carefully orchestrates its acts and attitudes to prepare young men and women for citizenship. At our very best, everything we do and say aims at building respect for each other, at fostering a civility of discourse that is the hallmark of a good college as well as the nursery of responsible citizenship. We cherish an enormous tolerance of individual differences, of the burdens and risks of personal responsibility, in other words of each other as free and independent human beings. We teach the young that a man or woman earns respect principally by giving it. Mandatory drug testing without proven cause is profoundly disrespectful. It is a bad lesson for universities to teach, and wretched training for citizens.

Timothy S. Healy, *The Washington Post National Weekly Edition*, September 15, 1986.

The state court sided with the students. It found, without analysis, that performing drug and alcohol tests on students' urine samples constituted a search. Then, relying on the U.S. Supreme Court's 1985 decision in *New Jersey v. T.L.O.*, the court held that the search was not supported by reasonable suspicion:

Assuming arguendo, that this is strictly and solely a medical examination to inquire into a medical condition, a position which this court does not accept, I would still find that the activities [of the school officials] violate the reasonable privacy expectations of school children. . . . The raw numbers and percentages of students referred to student counseling as compared with the total student body [are] not reasonably related in scope to the circumstances which justify the interference, urinalysis, in the first place.

Circumventing Due Process

The court also suggested that the drug tests might be an effort by school officials to circumvent the requirement that students be accorded due process prior to disciplinary action by the school. The court noted that school policy provided for suspension and expulsion of students as a disciplinary matter for drug activities only *after* a due process hearing. The court termed "unacceptable" any distinction between punishment under that policy and similar

treatment of students without due process "for medical reasons."
The court found that

> in light of the Board of Education's proposed use of
> urinalysis . . . , this court suggests that the spectrum of items
> that could be approached simply by defining them as medical
> is limitless. To accept [the school officials'] position suggests that
> medical testing is without limit. The Board of Education's use
> of an exclusion to prohibit class attendance which does not pro-
> vide for the due process mandated by [other cases] fails to pass
> constitutional muster.

Recognizing Statements That Are Provable

From various sources of information we are constantly confronted with statements and generalizations about social and moral problems. In order to think clearly about these problems, it is useful if one can make a basic distinction between statements for which evidence can be found and other statements which cannot be verified or proved because evidence is not available, or the issue is so controversial that it cannot be definitely proved.

Readers should constantly be aware that magazines, newspapers and other sources often contain statements of a controversial nature. The following activity is designed to allow experimentation with statements that are provable and those that are not.

Most of the following statements are taken from the viewpoints in this chapter. Consider each statement carefully. *Mark P for any statement you believe is provable. Mark U for any statement you feel is unprovable because of the lack of evidence. Mark C for statements you think are too controversial to be proved to everyone's satisfaction.*

If you are doing this activity as a member of a class or group, compare your answers with those of other class or group members. Be able to defend your answers. You may discover that others will come to different conclusions than you. Listening to the reasons others present for their answers may give you valuable insights in recognizing statements that are provable.

If you are reading this book alone, ask others if they agree with your answers. You will find this interaction very valuable.

P = *provable*
U = *unprovable*
C = *too controversial*

1. The President's Commission on Organized Crime spent 32 months and nearly five million dollars preparing its report on drug abuse and trafficking.

2. The administration hopes private companies will follow its example and begin random urinalysis programs for their employees.

3. All military personnel have been tested for drugs at least once since the Pentagon began drug testing in 1982.

4. Laboratory owners will be delighted with the trend toward drug testing.

5. The President showed his approval of drug testing by submitting voluntarily to urinalysis.

6. One-quarter of all Fortune 500 companies now administer urinalysis tests to applicants or current employees.

7. Drug tests are justified for air traffic controllers, but not for anyone else.

8. Eventually all employers will require urinalysis for prospective employees.

9. The drug tests employed in screening programs are never accurate enough to protect innocent workers.

10. Radioimmunoassay tests have yielded false positive rates of 43 percent in some studies.

11. A urine drug screen can register either falsely positive or falsely negative.

12. Today's younger generation will be overwhelmed by the problem of drug abuse if schools and parents do not take decisive action.

13. If employers make it clear that drug abusers will lose their jobs, drug abuse in the workplace will virtually cease.

14. Mandatory school drug testing should begin at the junior high level.

15. Some high schools have included random urinalysis in their programs to stop drug abuse among teenagers.

16. If school officials begin testing students for drugs, there is no limit to the liberties these students will lose for the sake of a "drug-free" society.

Periodical Bibliography

The following articles have been selected to supplement the diverse views expressed in this chapter.

Lawrence K. Altman	"Drug Tests Gain Precision, But Can Be Inaccurate," *The New York Times*, September 16, 1986.
Janice Castro	"Battling the Enemy Within," *Time*, March 17, 1986.
Jeffrey E. Fogel	"An Invasion of Privacy," *The New York Times*, November 10, 1985.
Hugh J. Hansen	"Crisis in Drug Testing," *Journal of the American Medical Association*, April 26, 1985.
William Hoffer	"Business' War on Drugs," *Nation's Business*, October 1986.
Irving R. Kaufman	"The Battle Over Drug Testing," *The New York Times Magazine*, October 19, 1986.
Dean Latimer	"The Test That Failed," *Inquiry*, May 1984.
Peggy Mann	"The Hidden Scourge of Drugs in the Workplace," *Reader's Digest*, February 1984.
Alfred L. Marbaise	"Treating a Disease," *The New York Times*, November 10, 1985.
Gary T. Marx	"Drug Foes Aren't High on Civil Liberties," *The New York Times*, February 24, 1986.
Tom Morganthau	"A Question of Privacy," *Newsweek*, September 29, 1986.
Jefferson Morley	"Our Puritan Dilemma," *The New Republic*, December 1, 1986.
The New Republic	"The Right Spirit," September 8, 1986.
William Serrin	"Drug Tests Promote Safety, Many Say," *The New York Times*, September 16, 1986.
USA Today	"Opinion Debate: Drugs and Travel," February 3, 1987.
Richard Vigilante	"Reaganites at Risk," *National Review*, December 5, 1986.
Michael Waldholz	"Drug Testing in the Workplace: Whose Rights Take Precedence?" *The Wall Street Journal*, November 11, 1986.

What Should Be Done About the Drug Problem in Sports?

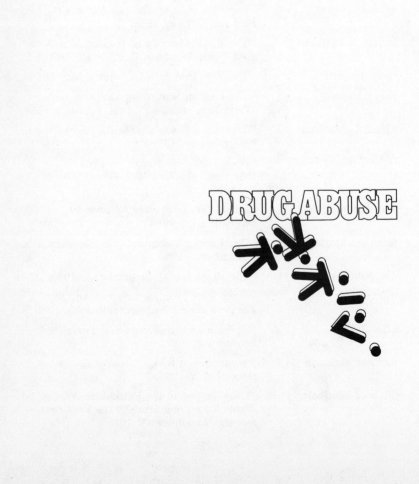

Chapter Preface

In June 1986 a young University of Maryland basketball star named Len Bias died of an overdose of cocaine. He was not the first athlete to die of a drug overdose, but his highly publicized death drew attention to the problem of drugs in sports.

Whether or not drug abuse is more pervasive in sports than in the general population is debatable, but it is a documented problem highlighted by the publicity spotlight on athletics. Both student and professional athletes have admitted to using recreational drugs to escape pressure and performance-enhancing drugs to increase their competitive advantage. Performance-enhancing drugs include steroids and growth hormones which many athletes believe build muscle size and strength. These drugs can be legally prescribed, unlike most narcotics, but they are often firmly condemned on the grounds that they are unhealthy and unethical.

Concern over drug abuse in sports is heightened by the fact that athletes are viewed as role models who can influence the actions of young people. Their lives are often subjected to greater scrutiny, including mandatory drug testing, to ensure that they are not setting a bad example. Some athletes and coaches rebel against this scrutiny. Others accept it as part of their responsibility.

Frank Layden, coach and general manager of the Utah Jazz, a professional basketball team, has said that to be "rich and young at the same time is the worst possible combination." College and professional athletes have ample means to purchase the narcotics their friends are using and the steroids their competitors are taking. The availability of these drugs to athletes and the variety of opinion on their appropriate uses ensures a continued debate on the problem of drugs in sports.

"The use of performance-enhancing drugs is ethically undesirable."

Drugs Should Be Banned from Sports

Thomas H. Murray

Thomas H. Murray is professor of Ethics and Public Policy at the Institute for the Medical Humanities at the University of Texas Medical Branch in Galveston, Texas. In the following viewpoint, he condemns the use of performance-enhancing drugs in sports, that is, the use of drugs like steroids that improve athletic performance. Murray believes such drugs should be prohibited because they can harm the athlete and because athletes are too often forced into using them.

As you read, consider the following questions:

1. How does Murray define "performance-enhancing drugs"? What common example does he give?
2. According to the author, why does the argument for personal liberty fail to justify drugs in sports?
3. Why does the author think performance-enhancing drugs are coercive?

Thomas H. Murray, "The Coercive Power of Drugs in Sports," *The Hastings Center Report*, August 1983. Reproduced by permission. © The Hastings Center.

Our images of the nonmedical drug user normally include the heroin addict nodding in the doorway, the spaced-out marijuana smoker, and maybe, if we know that alcohol is a drug, the wino sprawled on the curb. We probably do not think of the Olympic gold medalist, the professional baseball player who is a shoo-in for the Hall of Fame, or the National Football League lineman. Yet these athletes and hundreds, perhaps thousands of others regularly use drugs in the course of their training, performance, or both. I am talking not about recreational drug use—athletes use drugs for pleasure and relaxation probably no more or less than their contemporaries with comparable incomes—but about a much less discussed type of drug use: taking drugs to enhance performance.

Performance-Enhancing Drugs

It is a strange idea. Most of us think of drugs in one of two ways. Either they are being properly used by doctors and patients to make sick people well or at least to stem the ravages of illness and pain, or they are being misused—we say "abused"—by individuals in pursuit of unworthy pleasures. Performance-enhancing drug use is so common and so tolerated in some forms that we often fail to think of it as "drug" use. The clearest example is the (caffeinated) coffee pot, which is as much a part of the American workplace as typewriters and timeclocks. We drink coffee (and tea and Coke) for the "lift" it gives us. The source of "that Pepsi feeling" and the "life" added by Coke is no mystery—it is caffeine or some of its close chemical relatives, potent stimulants to the human central nervous system. Anyone who has drunk too much coffee and felt caffeine "jitters," or drunk it too late at night and been unable to sleep can testify to its pharmacological potency. Caffeine and its family, the xanthines, can stave off mental fatigue and help maintain alertness, very important properties when we are working around a potentially dangerous machine, fighting through a boring report, or driving for a long stretch.

Caffeine, then, is a performance-enhancing drug. Using caffeine to keep alert is an instance of the nonmedical use of a drug. So, too, is consuming alcohol at a cocktail party for the pleasure of a mild inebriation, or as a social lubricant to enable you to be charming to people you find intolerably boring when you are sober. In the first case, alcohol is a pleasure-enhancer; in the second, it is a performance-enhancer. What the drug is used for and the intention behind the use—not the substance itself—determines whether we describe it as medical or nonmedical; as pleasure-, performance-, or health-enhancing.

The area of human endeavor that has seen the most explosive growth in performance-enhancing drug use is almost certainly sport. At the highest levels of competitive sports, where athletes

129

strain to improve performances already at the limits of human ability, the temptation to use a drug that might provide an edge can be powerful. Is this kind of drug use unethical? Should we think of it as an expression of liberty? Or do the special circumstances of sport affect our moral analysis? In particular, should liberty give way when other important values are threatened, and when no one's good is advanced? These questions frame the discussion that follows. . . .

PLAYS FOR KEEPS

© Liederman/Rothco

May athletes use drugs to enhance their athletic performance? The International Olympic Committee [IOC] has given an answer of sorts by flatly prohibiting "doping" of any kind. This stance creates at least as many problems as it solves. It requires an expensive and cumbersome detection and enforcement apparatus, turning athletes and officials into mutually suspicious adversaries. It leads Olympic sports medicine authorities to proclaim that drugs like steroids are ineffective, a charge widely discounted by athletes, and thereby decreases the credibility of Olympic officials. Drug use is driven underground, making it difficult to obtain sound medical data on drug side effects.

The enforcement body, in an attempt to balance firmness with fairness, bans athletes "for life" only to reinstate them a year later, knowing that what distinguishes these athletes from most others is only that they were caught.

Any argument for prohibiting or restricting drug use by Olym-

130

pic athletes must contend with a very powerful defense based on our concept of individual liberty. We have a strong legal and moral tradition of individual liberty that proclaims the right to pursue our life plans in our own way, to take risks if we so desire and, within very broad limits, do with our own bodies what we wish. This right in law has been extended unambiguously to competent persons who wish to refuse even life-saving medical care. More recently, it has been extended to marginally competent persons who refuse psychiatric treatment. Surely, competent and well-informed athletes have a right to use whatever means they desire to enhance their performance.

Those who see performance-enhancing drug use as the exercise of individual liberty are unmoved by the prospect of some harm. They believe it should be up to the individual, who is assumed to be a rational, autonomous, and uncoerced agent, to weigh probable harms against benefits, and choose according to his or her own value preferences. It would be a much greater wrong, they would say, to deny people the right to make their own choices. Why should we worry so much about some probabilistic future harm for athletes while many other endeavors pose even greater dangers? High-steel construction work and coal-mining, mountain-climbing, hang-gliding, and auto-racing are almost certainly more dangerous than using steroids or other common performance-enhancing drugs.

Limiting Liberty

Reasons commonly given to limit liberty fall into three classes: those that claim that the practice interferes with capacities for rational choice; those that emphasize harms to self; and those that emphasize harm to others. The case of performance-enhancing drugs and sport illustrates a fourth reason that may justify some interference with liberty, a phenomenon we can call "inherent coerciveness." But first the other three reasons.

There is something paradoxical about our autonomy: we might freely choose to do something that would compromise our future capacity to choose freely. Selling oneself into slavery would be one way to limit liberty, by making one's body the property of another person. If surrendering autonomous control over one's body is an evil and something we refuse to permit, how much worse is it to destroy one's capacity to *think* clearly and independently? Yet that is one thing that may happen to people who abuse certain drugs. We may interfere with someone's desire to do a particular autonomous act if that act is likely to cause a general loss of the capacity to act autonomously. In this sense, forbidding selling yourself into slavery and forbidding the abuse of drugs likely to damage your ability to reason are similar *restrictions* on liberty designed to *preserve* liberty.

131

This argument applies only to things that do in fact damage our capacity to reason and make autonomous decisions. While some of the more powerful pleasure-enhancing drugs might qualify, no one claims that performance-enhancing drugs like the steroids have any deleterious impact on reason. This argument, then, is irrelevant to the case of performance-enhancing drugs. . . .

Harm to Others

A second class of reasons to limit liberty says that we may interfere with some actions when they result in wrong to others. The wrong done may be direct—lying, cheating, or other forms of deception are unavoidable when steroid use is banned. Of course, we could lift the ban, and then the steroid use need no longer be deceptive; it could be completely open to the same extent as other training aids. Even with the ban forcing steroids into the pale of secrecy, it would be naive to think that other athletes are being deceived when they all know that steroids are in regular use. The public may be deceived, but not one's competitors. There is no lie when no one is deceived. Using steroids may be more like bluffing in poker than fixing the deck, at least for your competitors.

Integrity of Sports

The integrity of the game is everything. We have to eliminate illegal substances from the game, substances that can be used to control people.

Peter Ueberroth, quoted in *Maclean's*, June 17, 1985.

The wrong we do to others may be indirect. We could make ourselves incapable of fulfilling some duty we have to another person. For example, a male athlete who marries and promises his wife that they will have children makes himself sterile with synthetic anabolic steroids (a probable side effect). He has violated his moral duty to keep a promise. This objection could work, but only where the duty is clearly identifiable and not overly general, and the harm is reasonably foreseeable. Duties to others must have a limited, clear scope or become absurdly general or amorphous. We may believe that parents have the duty to care for their children, but we do not require parents to stay by their children's bedside all night, every night, to prevent them from suffocating in their blankets. The duty is narrower than that. In order to avoid being too vague, we would have to be able to specify what the "duty to care for one's children" actually includes. Except for cases like the sterile athlete reneging on his promise, instances where athletes make themselves incapable of fulfilling some specific duty

132

to others would probably be rare. In any case, we cannot get a general moral prohibition on drug use in sports from this principle, only judgments in particular cases.

We may also do a moral wrong to others by taking unneccessary risks and becoming a great burden to family, society, or both. The helmetless motorcyclist who suffers severe brain damage in an accident is a prototype case. Increasingly, people are describing professional boxing in very similar terms. While this might be a good reason to require motorcyclists to wear helmets or to prohibit professional boxing matches, it is not a sound reason to prohibit steroid use. No one claims that the athletes using steroids are going to harm themselves so grievously that they will end up seriously brain-damaged or otherwise unable to care for themselves.

Free Choice Under Pressure

Olympic and professional sport, as a social institution, is an intensely competitive endeavor, and there is tremendous pressure to seek a competitive advantage. If some athletes are believed to have found something that gives them an edge, other athletes will feel pressed to do the same, or leave the competition. Unquestionably, coerciveness operates in the case of performance-enhancing drugs and sport. Where improved performance can be measured in fractions of inches, pounds, or seconds, and that fraction is the difference between winning and losing, it is very difficult for athletes to forego using something that they believe improves their competitors' performance. Many athletes do refuse; but many others succumb; and still others undoubtedly leave rather than take drugs or accept a competitive handicap. Under such pressure, decisions to take performance-enhancing drugs are anything but purely "individual" choices.

Can we say that "freedom" has actually been diminished because others are using performance-enhancing drugs? I still have a choice whether to participate in the sport at all. In what sense is my freedom impaired by what the other athletes may be doing? If we take freedom or liberty in the very narrow sense of noninterference with my actions, then my freedom has not been violated, because no one is prohibiting me from doing what I want, whether that be throwing the discus, taking steroids, or selling real estate. But if we take freedom to be one of a number of values, whose purpose is to support the efforts of persons to pursue reasonable life plans without being forced into unconscionable choices by the actions of others, then the coerciveness inherent when many athletes use performance-enhancing drugs and compel others to use the same drugs, accept a competitive handicap, or leave the competition can be seen as a genuine threat to one's life plan. When a young person has devoted years to reach the highest levels in an event, only to find that to compete successfully he or she must take potentially grave risks to health, we have as serious a threat to human flourishing as many restrictions on liberty.

The Value of Improved Performance

At this point it might be useful to consider the social value we place on improved performance in sport. It is a truism that you win a sports event by performing better than any of your competitors. The rules of sport are designed to eliminate all influences on the outcome except those considered legitimate. Natural ability, dedication, cleverness are fine; using an underweight shot-put, taking a ten-yard head start, fielding twelve football players are not. The rules of sport are man-made conventions. No natural law deems that shot-puts shall weigh sixteen pounds, or that football teams shall consist of eleven players. Within these arbitrary conventions, the rules limit the variations among competitors to a small set of desired factors. A willingness to take health risks by consuming large quantities of steroids is *not* one of the desired, legitimate differences among competitors.

Curbing Drug Abuse

It's high time that pro leagues and big-time college programs prove they are willing to pay the price—in personnel and possible embarrassment—that would be exacted if drug abuse is really curbed. And no more cracking down on drugs so *selectively*.

Rick Reilly, *Sports Illustrated*, July 14, 1986.

Changing the rules of a sport will alter performances, but not necessarily the standing of competitors. If we use a twelve-lb. shot-put, everyone will throw it farther than the sixteen-lb. one, but success will still depend on strength and technique, and the best at sixteen pounds will probably still be best at twelve pounds. Giving all shot-putters 10 mg. of Dianabol [a steroid] a day will have a similar impact, complicated by variations in physiological response to the drug. Noncatastrophic changes in the rules may shift some rankings, but will generally preserve relations among competitors. Changes that do not alter the nature of a sport, but greatly increase the risk to competitors are unconscionable. Changes that affirmatively tempt athletes to take the maximum health risk are the worst. Lifting the ban on performance-enhancing drugs would encourage just that sort of brinksmanship. On the other hand, an effective policy for eliminating performance-enhancing drug use would harm no one, except those who profit from it.

My conclusions are complex. First, the athletes who are taking performance-enhancing drugs that have significant health risks are engaging in a morally questionable practice. They have turned a sport into a sophisticated game of "chicken." Most likely, each athlete feels pressed by others to take drugs, and does not feel he or she is making a free choice. The "drug race" is analogous to the arms race.

Second, since the problem is systemic, the solution must be too. The IOC has concentrated on individual athletes, and even then it has been inconsistent. This is the wrong place to look. Athletes do not use drugs because they like them, but because they feel compelled to. Rather than merely punishing those caught in the social trap, why not focus on the system? A good enforcement mechanism should be both ethical and efficient. To be ethical, punishment should come in proportion to culpability and should fall on *all* the guilty parties—not merely the athletes. Coaches, national federations, and political bodies that encourage, or fail to strenuously discourage, drug use are all guilty. Current policy punishes only the athlete.

To be efficient, sanctions should be applied against those parties who can most effectively control drug use. Ultimately, it is the athlete who takes the pill or injection, so he or she ought to be one target of sanctions. But coaches are in an extraordinarily influential position to persuade athletes to take or not to take drugs. Sanctions on coaches whose athletes are caught using drugs could be very effective. Coaches, not wanting to be eliminated from future competitions, might refuse to take on athletes who use performance-enhancing drugs.

Ethically Undesirable

Finally, although I am not in a position to elaborate a detailed plan to curtail performance-enhancing drug use in sports, I have tried to establish several points. Despite the claims of individual autonomy, the use of performance-enhancing drugs is ethically undesirable because it is coercive, has significant potential for harm, and advances no social value. Furthermore, any plan for eliminating its use should be just and efficient, in contrast to current policies.

Can we apply this analysis of drug use in sports to other areas of life? One key variable seems to be the social value that the drug use promotes, weighed against the risks it imposes. If we had a drug that steadied a surgeon's hand and improved her concentration so that surgical errors were reduced at little or no personal risk, I would not fault its use. If, on the other hand, the drug merely allowed the surgeon to operate more quickly and spend more time on the golf course with no change in surgical risk, its use would be at best a matter of moral indifference. Health, in the first case, is an important social value, one worth spending money and effort to obtain. A marginal addition to leisure time does not carry anywhere near the same moral weight.

A careful, case-by-case, practice-by-practice weighing of social value gained against costs and risks appears to be the ethically responsible way to proceed in deciding on the merits of performance-enhancing drugs.

"To label performance-enhancing or additive drugs as unfair . . . is a policy without a justification."

Drugs Should Not Be Banned from Sports

Norman Fost

Norman Fost is the director of the Program in Medical Ethics at the University of Wisconsin. In spite of his personal distaste for drugs in sports, he contends in the following viewpoint that they should not be banned. Some drugs are acceptable, Fost says, and since it is impossible to distinguish between ethical and unethical uses of drugs, it is wrong to deny anyone their use. Society opposes drugs, according to Fost, because they violate our notions of acceptable behavior, but such opposition is not based on policies that make good ethical sense.

As you read, consider the following questions:

1. Why are present policies on drugs in sports ambiguous, according to Fost?
2. How does the author distinguish between "restorative" and "additive" drugs? What is another name for additive drugs?
3. According to the author, why isn't inequality unfair in sports?

Norman Fost, "Banning Drugs in Sports: A Skeptical View," *The Hastings Center Report*, August 1986. Reproduced by permission. © The Hastings Center.

Nearly everyone condemns the use of drugs—amphetamines, cocaine, steroids, and narcotics—in sports. But other drugs—antibiotics, insulin, vitamins, and aspirin—are quite acceptable. The basis for these distinctions is not obvious, nor is it self-evident why there should be any restrictions on the use of drugs in sports. Drugs can be used for various purposes: to restore a person with a disease to normal function; to improve function in a healthy person; to relieve pain; and to give pleasure, with no expected effects on performance.

Let me emphasize my personal distaste for drugs in sports, particularly performing-enhancing and recreational drugs. As an athlete, I would not use them. As a physician, I would not prescribe them. As a father, I would urge my children to avoid them. As a citizen, I deplore their widespread use. But these are merely preferences and not a sufficient basis for a national policy that claims to be based on ethical considerations.

Restorative or Performance-Enhancing?

In the 1972 Olympics, Rick DeMont, an American long-distance swimmer, had to give up a gold medal when it was discovered he had taken his routine antiasthmatic medications before the race. He apparently was unaware that the medicine contained a prohibited substance—ephedrine. Presumably the punishment was imposed for the procedural error of failing to comply with regulations, rather than for the substantive error of improperly enhancing performance.

It is probably irrelevant whether he took the banned drug to relieve an asthma attack and thereby restore his pulmonary function, or to gain whatever additive effect the ephedrine might provide. The presumed purpose of banning certain drugs was not to proscribe or punish bad intentions, but to prevent an athlete from gaining unfair advantage. DeMont's problem was complicated by the possible double-effect, restorative and additive, of ephedrine. But let me consider the premise that a drug with purely restorative actions—insulin, for example—would be permissible.

An Ambiguous Policy

The policy of allowing an athlete to use a drug that combats a disease, illness, or disability is ambiguous in two regards. First, it presupposes a consensus or rational basis for defining disease, and for distinguishing diseases that may acceptably be treated before competition from those that may not. Suppose, for example, an athlete suffering from the ailment "narcotic withdrawal" desired treatment to restore himself to a normal or baseline state. Apart from moralistic statements about the importance of not empathizing with such a disease, how can we distinguish such an illness from asthma, diabetes, or endogenous depression? One might point out its social or personal causation, rather than some intrinsic or uncontrollable etiology. Such a distinction would be specious, since many diseases and disabilities result from an interaction of volitional and involuntary forces. The asthmatic might not wheeze if he did not exercise, or if he stayed away from substances that provoked an attack.

Fans Expect Players To Party

The simple fact is this: fans expect players to party, like any other entertainers, like any other Americans, like themselves. And why shouldn't they? In America, opium (and more widely available substitutes, like cocaine, beer and marijuana) is the religion of the people.

Jamie Kitman, *The Nation*, April 26, 1986.

Second, and more important, allowing an athlete to restore his function to "normal" or "baseline" fails to address the ambiguity of those concepts. The Olympic athlete can hardly consider his strength or speed normal. In fact, his functioning in a diseased state may be closer to what we would generally consider normal. DeMont, wheezing or not, could swim laps around me. What the athlete seeks through restorative drugs is not normal function, in a statistical sense, but something closer to his personal baseline. But even personal baseline is not what the world-class athlete seeks. He wants to be beyond his baseline or normal level, preferably at a level of performance that is supernormal even for him. In these settings the distinction between restorative and additive is unclear.

Distinguishing Needs from Wants

One might try to distinguish restorative from additive drugs by distinguishing needs from wants. The restorative drug is presumably given because of a medical need; the additive drug is hardly needed in the medical sense, but is devoutly wanted as an adjunct to performance. This distinction also assumes an ability to distinguish wants from needs in a value-free way, as if these were purely medical judgments. The mild asthmatic does not need medication for normal daily functions, or to enjoy the pleasures of sport, or even to compete in a variety of contests other than world-class events. He uses drugs not because he is sick or disabled, but because being very good is not enough. He wants, not needs, to be as good as he possibly can be.

Similarly, the athlete who asks for anabolic steroids is commonly already a superhuman, but wants to be one notch better. If there is a distinction between a mild asthmatic and nonasthmatic Olym

139

pian, it is not that one is sick or subnormal. They are both "super-normal." The asthmatic is limited by pulmonary function that prevents him from achieving his maximal performance. The nonasthmatic might be limited by insufficient strength or speed. Neither seeks normality but both seek maximal possible performance. Suggesting that physical limitations that interfere with such maximization necessarily connote illness distorts our customary understanding of that concept.

Performance-Enhancing Drugs

Claims of additive powers of drugs are often exaggerated, based on hearsay, or, at the least, unproven. But some drugs, such as anabolic steroids, probably do enhance performance in some individuals. Why should effective additives be proscribed? The simple answer is that they give unfair advantage. There are two problems with this argument.

First, even if drugs did enhance performance, that alone would not be a sufficient reason for considering such enhancement unfair. Inequality *per se* is not unfair. Many endogenous and exogenous factors enhance performance without raising such concern. It is not unfair that Kareem Abdul-Jabbar is taller, quicker, and smarter than his opponents on a basketball court, or that Martina Navratilova is stronger and faster on the tennis court. Some of their superiority is earned, the reward for long hours of practice and the willingness to endure pain and other deprivations; but much of it is unearned, the result of unequal genetic endowment. No amount of commitment would enable most athletes to play professional sports. But since this genetic lottery is not the result of human choice, we do not usually consider it immoral, or perhaps even unfair.

In some sports, however, unequal genetic endowment is considered unfair. Boxers and wrestlers do not compete against bigger or stronger opponents. Considerable effort is invested in matching opponents by size. Then why not arrange events that reward speed or height so that the slow compete against the slow, the short against the short? The answer lies partly in the financial burden of underwriting fair competition in all areas. The public is not interested in a professional basketball league made up of six-footers. The existence of 150-pound football and separate women's leagues reflects an awareness that fair competition requires approximate matching according to genetic endowment.

Inequality and Unfairness

Questions of unfairness arise more commonly when inequality is the result of conscious human decisions, but that alone does not make inequality unfair. Much of Abdul-Jabbar's advantage results from his deliberate effort to gain such an advantage by practicing long hours. We do not consider such deliberate one-upsmanship immoral; it is the essence of fair competition. The challenge is to define the characteristics of unfair advantage. The current campaign to label performance-enhancing or additive drugs as unfair, without explaining why, is a policy without a justification.

Even if we were to concede, for the moment, that the use of some performance-enhancing drugs is unfair, there are inconsistencies that suggest confusion about which additives are permissible and why. Many exogenous "additives" are ingested with the specific intent of improving performance. Special diets, vitamins, fluids, electrolytes, and even placebos are lawfully ingested for the specific intent of improving performance. The distinction between the banned and the permitted is presumably not based on relative efficacy, since there is agreement that some legal substances enhance performance. Since all such substances are chemicals, we need some other basis for distinguishing good from bad.

Drugs a Part of Sports

America is a drug culture, so why should pro football be any different?

Tim Stokes, quoted in *Sports Illustrated*, August 15, 1983.

Nor does it help to distinguish foods from drugs, for the conventional definitions do not do so. The FDA defines a drug as ".... articles (other than food) intended to affect the structure or any function of the body." Food means "articles used for food," a tautology of no help here.

If the concern for exogenous additives were centered on fairness, we could avoid the problem by making efficacious substances available to all. Legalizing all drugs, or even distributing them free at the training table or at game time, would moot charges of unfairness. Athletes would be free to eschew such aids, just as they are free to avoid training hard, or risking injury through weight-training. However, they could no longer claim their opponents' advantage was unfair.

The Risk Argument

If the unfairness argument fails, perhaps there is another rational basis for prohibiting certain drugs, or for distinguishing the banned from the permitted. Perhaps the banned list is considered more toxic, but such a paternalistic justification would require considerable argument and would be disingenuous. In many sports, the risk of competing is greater than the risk of taking certain banned substances. We cannot plausibly argue that we prohibit

141

professional football players from using steroids or amphetamines because of concern for their health, when the sport itself permanently disables a high proportion of participants. The number of deaths from boxing, football, or auto racing far exceeds even the speculative harms from presently used drugs. Yet those who are most concerned about the harms of drug use are relatively tolerant of these more dangerous activities.

Even if toxicity from drugs exceeded harm from the sport itself, it would be beside the point. We tolerate the high risk of some sports because spectators and participants enjoy them. We also tolerate death and disability because of the high value we place on autonomy and personal freedom. Whether or not a competent person seeks pleasure or financial gain involving risk is a personal decision. So long as the activity is not imposing burdens involuntarily on others, we reject paternalistic interference with risky behavior. Many jobs and recreational pursuits involve risks, often death, but most people would oppose regulations prohibiting competent persons from weighing those risks and benefits according to their own values.

The Coercion Argument

Sometimes the concern for toxicity shifts from pure paternalism to a claim that world-class athletes are not really free to choose and need protection from a system that forces them to take drugs. According to this view, athletes are required to keep up with competitors' techniques if they want to compete effectively. Calling this situation coercion fails to distinguish between an offer and a threat. Coercion normally refers to situations in which a person will be worse off by failing to act in the suggested way. An example is the person confronted by a robber who demands: "Your money or your life."

Athletes confronting the choice of whether to use steroids face an opportunity to be better than they are, admittedly at some risk, but with no loss of property, health, or basic rights if they refuse. The worst consequence is that they might fail to gain some extraordinary honor, such as a gold medal or a financial reward. Great opportunities are typically accompanied by extraordinary demands and risks. We would not lament for the athlete who complains he wants to win a gold medal in the discus but doesn't want to endure the risks of weight-lifting, or the swimmer who says she doesn't want the social costs of practicing long hours. Imagine a candidate for professional football who argues he is being coerced into risking knee injury. Such individuals are free to refuse these opportunities and attendant risks with no loss of anything to which they are entitled.

It is certainly true, as Thomas Murray points out, that "it is very difficult for athletes to forego using something that they believe improves their competitors' performance" and that "under such pressure, decisions to take performance-enhancing drugs are anything but purely 'individual' choices." However, these difficulties and pressures are inherent in all risk-taking decisions. In trying to define the limits of permissible pressures, Murray concludes: "When . . . . to compete successfully (a person) must take potentially grave risks to health, we have as serious a threat to human flourishing as many restrictions on liberty." This, of course, describes the decision to participate in sport as well as the decision to use additive drugs.

What Argument Is Left?

What, then, is left as a rational basis for opposing additive drugs? The inchoate feeling remains that there is an important distinction between "natural" and "unnatural" assists. Ideally, we want athletic competition to be based on intrinsic qualities, such as speed, strength, endurance, and character. Unnatural chemicals, it is claimed, obscure or diminish the importance of the "real" person. Even a horse race is less interesting if we know that one of the entrants (or all of them) is doped. But this feeling does not explain why many unnatural drugs are on the acceptable list and some natural ones, such as testosterone, are banned. If marijuana enhanced performance, we would not be persuaded to allow it just because it grows in the athlete's garden. Nor do we oppose the use of manufactured vitamins.

No Worse than Others

Athletes are no worse than policemen, doctors, psychologists, clergymen or newspapermen when it comes to booze and drugs. Doctors still lead the pack in drug abuse, and I'd rather see a drug user swinging a baseball bat than taking out my appendix.

Bill Little, quoted in *Sports Illustrated*, August 15, 1983.

While the yearning for natural competition is understandable and possibly laudable, it does not explain the present distinctions between banned and permitted drugs. The training techniques and diets used by athletes are unnatural in many ways, some of which have come to be accepted after initial resistance. The use of a fiberglass pole instead of a bamboo pole by pole-vaulters was initially resisted because of the obvious advantage it gave to those who had it. The response was not to ban it, but to make it available to everyone. This produced a different sport, perhaps less natural than its predecessor, but not one that is inherently immoral.

Some athletes say, "If I lose, I want it to be because my opponent is better than I, not because of some chemicals he took." Consider a special diet, developed by a nutritional scientist, proven to enhance performance. Would we suggest that victories aided by such a diet were corrupt, or that athletes who used such information to enhance their performance were immoral? Would it matter whether the diet used "artificial" food, made in factories and packaged in cans, or "natural" foods, eaten fresh from the farm, with or without chemical fertilizers? Would we establish testing procedures to ensure no athlete used such a diet? The difference between this kind of chemical assistance and drugs is unclear.

There is another sense in which drugs may be considered unnatural; namely, that they distort the nature of the sport. The rules of sport are, of course, not natural but man-made conventions. Many innovations have altered a sport more radically than drugs: the fiberglass vaulting pole, the lively baseball, and the elimination of the center jump after each field goal in basketball. It would be meaningless to talk of these alterations in moral terms. If we were genuinely concerned about changes that distort the nature of football and increase the risk, we might concentrate on the forward pass.

3

"I do understand individual rights, but given the problem at hand, the testing is justified."

Athletes Should Be Tested for Drugs

Thomas Boswell

Thomas Boswell is a columnist for the *Washington Post*. The following viewpoint is excerpted from interviews he conducted with a panel of professional and college coaches. All of the coaches quoted here are in favor of mandatory random drug testing for their athletes. The coaches agree that the drug problem is serious enough to justify testing and that mandatory testing is often the only way to help players who have become addicted to drugs.

As you read, consider the following questions:

1. What reasons do the coaches give for favoring mandatory rather than voluntary testing?
2. According to the coaches, what does drug testing do for the players?
3. How do the coaches respond to the charge that athletes succumb to drugs because they are under too much pressure?

Thomas Boswell, "Drug Tests: The View from Courtside," *Playboy*, February 1987. Copyright © 1986 by PLAYBOY.

The death of college star athlete Len Bias and the resultant resignation of University of Maryland coach Lefty Driesell suddenly sharpened debate on just who's accountable for drug abuse on the basketball court. To assess the risks—of both drugs and drug tests—*Washington Post* columnist Thomas Boswell grilled an all-star panel of pro and college coaches.

Jim Valvano, Head Basketball Coach, North Carolina State

When I was coaching the freshman team at Rutgers in 1967, if you'd told me that in 20 years the most important issue for a coach would not be how to break a zone press but whether or not to institute drug testing, I'd have said you were nuts. But that's exactly where we are.

Athletics gets too much ink in the newspapers, for good or for bad. But because of that, we can be leaders on the drug problem. We can make headline news—on the front page, and not just in the sports section. We should demand that our athletes be students and that they be drug-free. I am in favor of mandatory drug testing.

What surprises me is the amount of resistance to drug testing by people who say that it's a violation of individual freedoms. We're not talking about prayer in school here, we're talking about life and death. Everyone is trying to express the problem graphically, but nothing can be more graphic than seeing a talented player like Len Bias end his life at 22. I do understand individual rights, but given the problem at hand, the testing is justified.

We've had a drug-testing program at North Carolina State, but it's been voluntary. We in the athletic department think that mandatory drug testing is appropriate, and we want to enforce it strictly. On the first offense, the player is *gone*. We aren't a rehab program, and we aren't saying that certain substances are OK. We have 24 varsity sports here, and not one coach has a dissenting opinion.

We've just completed our first round of random drug testing and we haven't had one athlete, male or female, test positive. But you temper that with the knowledge that the most important drug we're trying to catch—cocaine—is the most difficult one to test for.

That's why the faculty members here are not quite sure whether or not they want drug testing. Marijuana remains in your system for a long time, so if somebody smokes a joint in December and you test him in late January, you're going to catch him. But cocaine goes through your system in 36 hours. So you can spend big money on tests that tell you your players are drug-free, and they may not be.

There's a lot of speculation about what causes the drug problem. Is it pressure? I haven't seen that with the kids I've coached. These kids grow up with pressure. If you're a good basketball player, that's established when you're a high school freshman, and you're

146

going to live with guys like me coming from all over the country to watch you play. Athletes today are more mature because of that.

The kids are still playing a game and enjoying it. [Former North Carolina State star] Spud Webb said that the place he feels most at home is on a basketball court. Everyone wants to put the blame on this "win at all costs" ethic of coaching, but kids can cope with winning and losing better than anything else they have to cope with. Maybe the pressure comes afterward, in social situations and media situations. Maybe we have to prepare kids better for their lives off the court. . . .

Red Auerbach, General Manager, Boston Celtics

I've been an advocate of unannounced drug testing from day one. I know that it's an invasion of privacy, but there comes a time when you've got to put this altruistic civil rights stuff down the toilet, find out who's using drugs and take it from there.

An Important Deterrent

The civil liberties objections to testing are serious. . . . But rigorous random testing . . . figures to be at least a partial deterrent to cocaine use. And with lives at stake, a partial deterrent is better than no deterrent at all. Testing should be tied to rehabilitation programs, but it should also have teeth. If a college kid fails a test once, for instance, his season is over—not his scholarship, his season—and into rehab he goes. If one member of a team fails a test at a championship event, the *team's* season is over. That might get a few coaches' attention.

Rick Reilly, *Sports Illustrated*, July 14, 1986.

Athletes are targets because of their leadership. Drug sellers approach them in 50 ways, because they know that if they get an athlete hooked, other students will say, "Hey, if my hero does it, what the hell; I may as well do it, too."

That's why it's so important to have drug tests. If a player starts in with drugs, you can spot it early, call him in, have a long chat and change his whole mode of life. And more drug tests should be done on a high school or even junior high school level. A high school athlete is less mature and less aware of the ramifications of getting involved, so he's a better target. When the kid goes from there to college, the contact has already been made.

I'm not a great believer in the psychiatric approach to drug counseling. I do think college players are entitled to some help with their schoolwork because of the amount of time they spend away from class. If somebody counted the number of days that players miss because of practice, road trips, tournaments, charitable appearances and TV, it would really add up. They've got to have somebody to help out. That's why [Georgetown's] John Thompson and [Indiana's] Bobby Knight are so great. They tell their players, "Hell, we won't let you go; that's all."

Colleges should also give athletes five years on scholarship to complete their coursework, because of the unusual demands on their time. For example, if a team makes the Final Four in basketball, the players are out pretty near a month. That's ridiculous. Unless the guys are geniuses, it's impossible for them to keep up with their studies. Len Bias failed, and people made a big issue of it. Everybody blamed Lefty, but there wasn't anything he could do about it. There was no way the kid could get to class.

The thing to do about the drug problem is to continue building awareness, so that the ballplayers will know that they'd better watch their step. You've got to make the penalty for taking drugs strong enough, because the biggest deterrent is fear: fear of not getting a scholarship to play ball, fear of being thrown off the team, fear of being deprived of a professional career.

Denny Crum, Head Basketball Coach, University of Louisville

To our knowledge, we've never had a drug problem at Louisville, but that doesn't mean we couldn't. We've instituted a prevention program, and we drug tested on a random basis. We have our own equipment, and we'll continue to use it. . . .

We also had a professional group that does drug prevention and rehabilitation work spend 16 hours in a seminar with our team. . . . I was not in the meetings—this was just between the professionals and the players. They talk about all aspects of drug abuse: what it does, what people think it does, how to say no, how to know when somebody is involved.

Education will make the difference. I'm really pleased to see the President and Nancy Reagan make a public issue of it. I think that it in itself could help. And to me, that's a step in the right direction. When they get behind something, I think people will fall in line.

Jerry Tarkanian, Head Basketball Coach, University of Nevada, Las Vegas

You need drug testing. I don't think you can continue to have intercollegiate athletics or even professional athletics if the paying customer doesn't trust the kids who are playing. I certainly wouldn't want to see a pro team playing and find out that the guys were on drugs.

We're in our third year of random drug testing at UNLV. The first time we did it was when school started, and three kids tested positive. They went home for the summer, got caught up with their friends and made a mistake.

The first time that happens, we bring the kid in for consultation. The second time, we notify his parents. The third time the player tests positive, he's suspended for the season. It's never gotten to the third time for any of our players.

Larry Brown, Head Basketball Coach, University of Kansas

We've been giving drug tests at Kansas, and that worries me. I always tell the kids I trust them, and here I am testing them for drugs. But if drug tests help prevent drug use, you've got to be in favor of them. I understand the right of privacy, but I'm not talking about that. I'm talking about stopping kids from doing something that can lead to deaths like Lenny Bias'.

The Need for Drug Testing

The National Collegiate Athletic Association says drug tests will insure fairness in championship play. Drug testing, it says, is just one more eligibility requirement. College athletes already meet academic standards and financial tests to assure they are amateurs. . . .

The need seems clear. In recent years Len Bias, the basketball All American, died from cocaine abuse; Tulane basketball players were accused of shaving points for money and drugs, and coaches at two universities were accused of providing steroids. Thirty-two players on football bowl teams last fall tested positive for steroids or other proscribed drugs.

The New York Times, March 7, 1987.

We have a doctor and a laboratory that administer the test. They pick the kids at random. I'm trying to change that. We're going to take them all, but the dates will be staggered so that they won't know when they're coming up. The first time a player tests positive, the trainer notifies him and he goes for counseling. The second time, he goes for more counseling, the family and coach are notified and he's suspended, but he retains his scholarship. The third time it comes up positive, he's suspended and he loses his scholarship. But I don't think we would carry out the third step. I think that we would try to stay with the kid as long as we could.

Drugs were just becoming popular when I started coaching. I watched some of the greatest young players do drugs and I was not able to help. [Former Denver Nuggets star] David Thompson and I had an unbelievable relationship. Then he got involved with drugs and became distant. At the time, I didn't know what the problem was, and when I found out, it was almost too late. Kids who are on drugs won't allow you to help them. They've got to make up their minds themselves. With [former New Jersey Nets player] Michael Ray Richardson, I was a little bit more aware. I helped take him to the hospital in New Jersey, but he was already gone.

Before these guys started on drugs, our relationships were real strong. Then, after the drug use started, I'd see them becoming distant from me and their teammates. I saw a tremendous deterioration in them physically, in both their appetites and their losses of weight and coordination. The thing that hurts is that when I was coaching at UCLA, the kids who remembered David would say, "Hey, this guy's the greatest." But he changed. I call David all the time, asking him to come back to work with us at Kansas, but we can't even reach the guy. . . .

I get really mad when I hear the charge that our basketball players are under too much pressure. I think that comes from a bunch of administrative guys who are making an excuse, saying we spend too much time with the kids. The kids love to play. I don't think they feel pressure and I don't think pressure is put on them. This is the greatest experience of their lives.

4

"The clubs have no rights whatsoever to try and force a kid to agree to random testing."

Testing Athletes Is Unfair

Bryan Burwell

Many college and professional athletic programs have initiated drug testing for their players. Some players have complied; others have objected. Bryan Burwell, who writes about the National Football League [NFL] for the New York *Daily News,* thinks the policy is unfair. In the following viewpoint he tells the story of one athlete who was branded as a drug addict without cause and now faces a loss of reputation and income. Drug testing, according to Burwell, is one more way for the athletic clubs to exploit their players and should not be permitted.

As you read, consider the following questions:

1. How were the results of the rookies' drug tests leaked, according to Burwell?
2. According to the author, why does the NFL management purposely leak drug test results to the press?
3. What effect does Burwell believe the leaked information will have on rookies?

Bryan Burwell, "Branded," *Sport*, August 1986. © Sport Magazine, 1986.

The little boy dreamed little-boy dreams. Like most young boys, those dreams took him on fantasy trips into the world of professional football. "Lord, wouldn't it be great," he thought, "to be in the NFL, *The National Football League*. Yeah, wouldn't that be something."

Well, now he's here, and he was right. It sure was something. Something else. The little boy's sweet dream had curdled like a sour glass of milk. What should have been all fun and games was now nothing but serious, distasteful business.

People were saying all sorts of things about him now. The wrong things. Or maybe he just thought they were saying things.

"Man, it was just rotten," the kid says. "Just rotten. I'd walk into a crowded room and just feel people were staring at me and whispering. I'd swear they were all looking and whispering, 'drug addict.'"

Testing Positive

This is the kid's story. He is among the 57 college players who tested positive during the drug tests at the NFL scouting combine rookie workouts in New Orleans. He is also among the 26 on that list who were drafted by NFL clubs.

He is also one of the four rookies who tested positive on those drug tests and found his test results—results that were supposed to have been a matter of privacy between the 28 NFL teams and the individual players—being revealed all over the country, either shortly before or shortly after the NFL draft.

So now when he and the three other rookies head into their respective NFL training camps this month to begin their professional careers, they will be carrying an extra burden. They will have been publicly labeled as drug users.

Private Information

"I still don't understand how it happened," says the kid, who, on the advice of his attorney, chose anonymity in telling his story. "They told us it was private information—just for the NFL teams. I figured since the clubs were paying for it, they were the only ones who would know about it. But when my name came out in the newspapers, I was angry. I felt betrayed."

The names became public because someone in the NFL leaked bits of information first to *The Boston Globe* and later to *The New York Times*. To the reporters' credit, neither paper printed the names of the players. Instead, what came out was a list of the 16 teams who drafted them. But, before long, a lot of people who shouldn't have been revealing names on that list were doing so. Strictly off the record, of course.

Because of the leaks from NFL management, four players have been branded, NFL-style.

- James FitzPatrick, Southern California. First-round draft pick by the San Diego Chargers. His name was made public two days after the draft, when Chargers president Alex Spanos—a staunch supporter of mandatory drug testing—told a reporter for the *Times Advocate* in Escondido, California, that FitzPatrick tested positive for marijuana. Spanos said he thought the conversation was totally off the record and not for publication. Within a day, the story was national news.

- Alonzo Johnson, Florida. Second-round draft pick by the Philadelphia Eagles. This is a strange tale, since no one has made any on-the-record confirmation about Johnson. However, long before the draft, Johnson's name was connected to drug-related rumors. By the time the draft rolled around, Johnson—once considered a certain first-round pick—found himself dropped to the early second round, where the Eagles took a chance on him. If Philadelphia hadn't taken the gamble, there's no telling how low Johnson might have slipped in the draft.

Unfair Attitudes

Why is the public so outraged when some quarterback or third baseman is picked up on a cocaine charge? When a John Belushi self-destructs, there is no outcry for the drug testing of actors. Outrage, it seems, is reserved for sports. When *Sports Illustrated* polled 2,000 adults about their views on sports, it was no surprise 73 percent of the respondents favored drug testing. A wonderful follow-up question to anyone who favors testing for athletes is whether that person would accept such examinations as a condition for employment. It also would be interesting to poll the members of the baseball, basketball, football and hockey writers associations to see if their members would submit to random drug testing.

Sandy Padwe, *The Nation*, September 27, 1986.

- Barry Word, Virginia. Third-round pick by the New Orleans Saints. Someone told the *New Orleans Times-Picayune* that Word had tested positive at the scouting combine. Later, Word admitted that he tested positive for marijuana use.

- Arnold Franklin, North Carolina. Eleventh-round pick by the Miami Dolphins. An unnamed source told the *Miami Herald* that Franklin tested positive for traces of marijuana. Franklin later admitted he had flunked the drug test.

A Cloud of Innuendo

These are the only rookies who have seen their names in the sports pages, but at least six or seven more—including two first-round picks—also will go to training camp with a heavy cloud of innuendo hanging over their heads. No one has confirmed in the media that these players tested positive, but that hasn't stopped anyone from whispering their names.

"And now you know why I don't want the owners or anyone connected with the teams to have control over these so-called 'confidential' drug tests," says NFL Players Association [NFLPA] executive director Gene Upshaw. "They want us to have mandatory drug testing, but how in the world can we trust them not to tell the whole world the test results? The answer is, you can't trust them."

Why this distrust between players and management? According to Upshaw and attorneys representing some of the branded rookies, there is a method to management's habit of leaking names:

Management's Method

• To prove to the public that the drug problem in pro football is not the NFL's fault. "They want you to believe they've inherited the problem," says one attorney. "They want everyone to think that the drug problems for these guys started long before they ever played in the NFL."

• A negotiating tool. "Think about it," Upshaw says. "It's a great control issue when they want to sit down and handle the negotiations on this player's contract. These rookies have their names spread across the sports pages as drug users and then their agents walk into the room to try and negotiate a contract. What kind of leverage do they have?"

• Another way of gaining the public's sympathy in the NFL Management Council's battle with the NFLPA on the random-drug-testing issue. "If this player tests positive and everyone knows about it," says Upshaw, "during negotiations, the owner will say, 'Look, we know you had a problem and that gives us reasonable cause to ask for random testing.' The kid doesn't know any better and wants to clear up his name, so he agrees to do it. But 'reasonable cause' doesn't begin until the player shows up at minicamp, not at that combine camp. The clubs have no rights whatsoever to try and force a kid to agree to random testing."

Even some club representatives agree that there was nothing voluntary about the way the tests were presented to the players. "We brought in a guy before the draft and for some reason he was unable to piss in a bottle," says an NFL player personnel director. "Maybe it was nerves, maybe it wasn't. But it does make you worry. It's the same as someone refusing to come in and have his knee tested. You're not going to take a chance on him either."

Powerless

The kid is totally confused and still a bit angry. "I felt like I had no power in the situation," says the kid. "I mean, how can I tell the NFL I wasn't going to take those tests at the combine? They had all the power. We had absolutely none. I mean, we're the ones who want to get into the NFL, so how many of us were going to tell them no?

"And now I'm stuck in the middle of a battle between the union and management. I want to clear my name up. I'd do anything to clear my name up, because it was only for marijuana anyway. But the union is telling me that I shouldn't agree to random testing and [the owner of the team he plays for] is saying, 'You'd better.' I don't know what's going on."

The kid isn't alone. According to descriptions of how the drug tests were conducted at the New Orleans scouting combine, it was clear that this was new ground for everyone—and the inexperience showed.

No Supervision

Players say that there was little control or supervision over the urinalysis. "They just handed us a bottle and we all stood in line waiting our turn," says one player. "Sometimes they had someone watching us, sometimes they didn't." There were reports that some players had others urinate in their bottles.

John Trever. Reprinted with permission.

There were reports that traces of codeine, a regular pharmaceutical medicine, showed up and was put on the chart as "CO." As a result, several players were briefly labeled as cocaine users.

Specialists in the field feel that a truly effective drug testing procedure—one that would both serve the needs of management and the wants of the players' union—would have to be conducted at a totally independent and confidential drug testing facility. The test results would then be reviewed by drug experts and they alone would determine whether the player had a serious abuse problem or if he merely had a brief experiment with marijuana.

They alone would determine whether the player's test results warranted release to clubs interested in drafting him. They alone would determine whether the player needed drug rehabilitation. They alone would control the list and insure the confidentiality of the situation.

"But the real tragedy is that none of that will help any of these players," says Upshaw. "Their reputations have already been ruined. It's not fair."

The damage has been done both financially and personally. Johnson's attorney, David Ware, estimates that his client lost between $500,000 and $600,000 in salary and bonuses as a result of falling from the first round to the early second round.

"And how about what this does for a player's endorsements or, more important, how he is perceived in the community?" says FitzPatrick's attorney, Leigh Steinberg. "All kids make mistakes. James made a mistake. But is the price he's paying really fair?"

Anger and Remorse

The kid is sitting in his hotel room at rookie minicamp. He is feeling remorse. But the remorse is fighting a battle with anger, and the kid isn't quite sure which emotion is winning.

"The day it all came out, my agent told me the next day it would be national news, spread all over the country," says the kid. "I went to bed knowing what it felt like to be a condemned man. Tonight I would go to bed a normal guy; tomorrow I'd be a drug addict. My friends tried to help me, tell me it was going to be all right, but it wasn't. My grandparents knew, my friends knew, everyone knew. I felt like a leper.

"Look, I'm not saying what I did was right, because it wasn't. I smoked some grass. I gave in. I was real depressed at the time. I was wrong. I shouldn't have done it, and now I'm paying for it. But this was supposed to be a private matter—between me and the team, that's all. Now everyone thinks I'm a drug addict and I'm not. But I don't think anyone will ever believe the truth."

===

"The drugs [steroids] are not harmful if taken under supervision and I prescribe them for those wishing to take them."

===

Steroids Should Be Allowed

Anthony P. Millar

Steroids are a natural male hormone produced at puberty to aid muscle development and bone growth. Many athletes believe that taking additional steroids will increase their size and strength and thus improve their athletic performance. Physicians, however, have issued warnings about possible dangerous side effects. In the following viewpoint, Dr. Anthony P. Millar, the founder and director of the Research Institute of Sports Medicine at Lewisham Hospital in Sydney, Australia, explains his policy of prescribing steroids to athletes who want to use them. He states that steroids are not immoral and are not harmful if properly administered.

As you read, consider the following questions:

1. Why does Millar think the use of anabolic steroids is inevitable?
2. According to the author, what is the most important factor in comparing results of the use of steroids?
3. What is the author's rationale for prescribing steroids?

Anthony P. Millar, "Anabolic Steroids: Should They Be Used To Improve Athletic Performance?" *Current Therapeutics*, October 1985. Reprinted with permission.

Athletes have always searched for a substance to elevate their performance levels above all other competitors' efforts. Since the Second World War, due to the worldwide growth in interest in sport and athletic achievements, there has been an upsurge in the use of chemical substances whether normally present in the body, such as vitamins, steroids etc., or as extraneous preparations, for example amphetamines, to improve performance. The variety of ergogenic aids is constantly being expanded. As a further factor, there has been a change in the moral values of those in the top echelons of sport, i.e. athletes, coaches and administrators, and now winning is the only thing that counts.

It was inevitable in this context that use would be made of drugs which increased muscle power and bulk such as anabolic steroids. [H. A.] Haupt and [G. D.] Rovere (1984) recorded that anabolic steroids were first used by the Russians in 1954. Since then they have been consumed by athletes in many, if not all, countries where power sports are performed. Their initial use was in weightlifting, but the results were soon carried over into those sports where power output was the measure of success.

There has been much controversy regarding the benefits of anabolic steroids. Athletes believe the drugs work—that is their single greatest benefit—and they know who the successful participants are who use them. Medical advisers decry their use as not effective and dangerous, but when athletes see results their path to success is abundantly clear. The drugs are banned by all amateur sporting groups; this in the athletes' eyes could only be because they are effective and this further stimulates their use. Testing at competitions does not prevent their use as they can be taken up to 4 to 6 weeks before competition with little chance that any will be detected at the time of winning. The dilemma as it exists now has 2 main aspects:

1) Do they work?
2) Are they dangerous?

Effects of Steroids

Naturally-produced steroids at puberty in the male cause development of secondary sex characteristics, deepen the voice, lead to muscular development and an increased rate of bone growth. . . . They also lead to change in the psychological perceptive of an individual. . . . This change plus the alteration in bone and muscle mass and red cells are the desired features of the anabolic steroid. To date, no purely anabolic agent is available; they all have androgenic [male-producing] features in their actions.

Review of the literature on anabolic steroids leads to widespread differences of opinion, with the route of administration being the most important factor when comparing results. Dose for dose, parenteral [outside the intestine] administration is more effective

158

than the oral route as oral preparations are partly detoxified in the liver leaving less material for anabolism.

The effects of anabolic steroids are dose related and [C. D.] Kochakian (1976) found no significant differences between the overall effects of different steroids once equivalent doses were given. The anabolic effect of a constant dose tended to wear off after a period of time, probably due to increased competition from corticoids. However, this effect can be regained by increasing the dose. Once the drugs are ceased the tissue slowly breaks down due to increased catabolism, the rate of tissue break down depending upon the level of training maintained.

No Trouble with Steroids

Even though I was a state champion, I started taking steroids because I thought my progress was slowing.

I was 5 feet 5 inches tall and weighed 155 pounds. I could lift a total of 1,150 pounds in the three lifts the event requires.

Three years later, weighing 165, I won the U.S. senior power-lifting title with 1,425 pounds.

In all, I've won nine state titles, and I think I'd probably have won most of them without steroids. But there's no way I could have won that national title without them.

Used properly, they are no more of a threat to an adult than liquor is. I've known many people who've used them, and except for one national champion who took very large doses I don't know anyone who's had trouble.

Ron Hale, *USA Today*, January 5, 1987.

There have been over 2000 papers published on the effects of these steroids, and there have been several factors leading to the differing conclusions found by the authors; the placebo effect being an important factor. [G.] Ariel and [W.] Saville (1972) presented a group of weightlifters with an opportunity to use the drug. They offered the best of their lifters a course of steroids after 8 weeks training. Following this their rate of improvement increased dramatically. The authors then disclosed that the 'drug' was actually a placebo thus revealing the impact on results of the name 'anabolic steroid.'

Conducting Tests of Steroids

Double-blind trials have been difficult to carry out due to the motivational effects of the anabolic steroids. Athletes taking the drugs experience euphoria and diminished fatigue which enhances training, and this effect is maintained whilst the drug is continued.

These easily perceived benefits have made it a simple matter for protocols to be broken thus destroying the double-blind basis as far as the athlete is concerned, if not the observer. Furthermore, the dose of steroid given is relevant to the results produced. However, the dose used in most trials does not approach that commonly accepted by athletes as the dose necessary for full benefit and this increases the credibility gap in this area.

The training state of the athletes at the time of commencing the trial is very important. In their review of the literature, Haupt and Rovere found a significant correlation between athletes who had weight trained before taking the drug and increased strength development, and a similar correlation between athletes who had not weight trained and the failure to gain strength. As all athletes in the first group had continued their training programme whilst on the drug, it was the combination of drug and training that caused the increase in strength.

A major problem facing investigators studying anabolic steroids has been to determine how to test strength. Some investigators have used a one repetition maximum effort (1RM), while others have used a 'Cybex' test programme, grip dynamometers, strain gauges and other methods of assessment. This leads to confusion. The technique of measurement for the best results must equate with the training programme which in turn must be related to the sport involved.

The Importance of Protein

It is obvious that nutrition plays a part in the strength developed as a result of training. The heavily trained lifter requires 2.2g/kg bodyweight of protein daily to prevent a negative nitrogen balance. Most athletes participating in this sport are conscious of this need and protein intake is often high, but it may not be quite enough and some are in a chronic state of imbalance. An athlete in negative nitrogen balance would benefit from anabolic drugs quite significantly as more protein would be incorporated into his system leading to gains in strength. . . .

Many of the already conducted steroid studies do not fulfil the generally accepted criteria for scientific experimentation. Reviewing the results shows an even split between enhanced strength and nil response, and although there is some bias towards strength improvement, a positive statement cannot be made on available data. The outstanding defect is that no data are available for the large doses that are used by today's athletes. It does appear, however, that if the drugs are to be prescribed, the athletes must be in weight training beforehand and must continue to work hard with the drugs, and in addition their protein intake must be adequate. . . .

The view expressed here is a personal one. The drugs are not

160

harmful if taken under supervision and I prescribe them for those wishing to take them. It is important that the athletes train to a high percentage of their capacity and maintain a good broadly-based diet. I initiate therapy with small doses over a 2-month period followed by a month without treatment and to date have continued this programme for 2 years without any significant side effects. The choice of steriod used is not important and the oral or parenteral route of administration is one of personal preference.

Not prescribing does not prevent the athlete taking the drug. It is not the taking that leads to dismissal, it is being caught. It is common knowledge among weightlifters that top level competitors use them up to 6 weeks or a month before competition and then cease or replace them with testosterone, a natural androgenic-anabolic steroid. In the present climate testing at monthly intervals is the safest way of maintaining health for those on steroids. Haemoglobin levels and liver function tests suffice.

No Different than Good Training

There's too much emphasis put on the role anabolic steroids play in the success of an athlete. It's really no different than having a good dietary program or training right. In the end the athlete's ability and his coaching decide whether he succeeds or not.

Robert Kerr, quoted in *The Washington Post*, August 10, 1984.

The decisions whether or not to prescribe must be based on the knowledge of the drug's actions, its side effects, and the stability of the athlete's intellectual faculties. The widespread use amongst males with little significant illness as a result confirms the safety of the drug. Whether it produces the results by its action on muscle or stimulates the athlete to train harder is undecided but certainly, in today's world where winning is the only goal, athletes will use steroids with or without our cooperation.

"In addition to our concern over the potential physical and psychological harm of steroid use, [we] consider the medically unjustified use of steroids as unethical and deplorable."

Steroids Should Not Be Allowed

The American College of Sports Medicine

The American College of Sports Medicine (ACSM) is the leading organization in sports medicine. It has published position stands and opinion statements concerning specific topics of interest. These scientific papers have been translated into lay format for the convenience of lay persons interested in health and physical fitness. ACSM states that the recommendations found in the summary are advisory only. The following viewpoint is a reprint of their lay summary on anabolic steroids.

As you read, consider the following questions:

1. According to the ACSM, what are the effects of steroids on humans? What are some of the undesirable effects?
2. Why does the ACSM take a stand against steroid use?

The anabolic steroids used by athletes are a group of powerful natural or synthetic compounds that are closely related chemically to the natural hormones of the male. Virtually every athlete, coach and trainer seriously interested in methods of increasing muscle size and strength is familiar with them. Since these drugs have generally been condemned by physicians and outlawed by sports federations, much of what is known by athletes is based on hearsay, personal contact and limited observation. Some athletes tend to view the effects as positive but in doing so are rather shortsighted.

A number of top athletes have publicly stated that they would do anything, even if it meant risking serious illness or death, to win in high-level competition. Unfortunately, the personal and financial stakes involved and the winner-take-all pattern of compensation have helped establish and reinforce the win-at-all-cost philosophy that seems to pervade sports. These factors, coupled with an increased availability of anabolic steroids, are associated with an increasing use of these substances to dangerous proportions.

Just what are these drugs and what do they do? As previously mentioned, anabolic steroids mimic the structure and effects of the male sex hormone (testosterone). Testosterone is called an "androgen" after the Greek word meaning "male producing." It is also "anabolic" in that it can stimulate the build up of tissue. Hence, these drugs are often referred to as "androgenic-anabolic" steroids. In this discussion only the word steroids will be used although it is recognized that there are many more steroids than the anabolic-androgenic steroids specifically referred to here.

Uses for Steroids

Scientists have met with success in changing the structure of some steroids in order to build muscle while minimizing the masculinizing effects of the hormone. However, no pure muscle-building steroid has yet been developed. All of the available drugs have both actions, but to varying degrees in different individuals.

The primary medical uses for these steroids include the following: 1) replacement therapy (for boys or men deficient in the natural male hormone); 2) malnutrition; 3) skeletal disorders and other growth deficiencies; 4) soft-tissue injuries; 5) certain types of anemia and wasting diseases; and 6) to offset the negative effects of radiation and chemotherapy treatment.

Many experiments have been carried out to identify the actions and effects of steroids. To date, studies involving normal healthy male animals such as rodents, dogs, cats, monkeys and domestic farm animals have been unable to demonstrate consistent positive effects of body weight or performance variables exceeding those resulting from regular exercise alone. Animals deficient in natural steroids (relative to young human males) often show substantial increases in muscular development with steroid administration. Unfortunately, application of animal performance data to human athletics, including strength sports, is difficult due to the lack of information on steroid interaction with prolonged and heavy weight training in animals.

Testing Steroids on People

The results of approximately 30 experiments have been published over the last two decades dealing with the effects of steroid use and exercise in human volunteers. In general, investigations showed that low doses of steroids used during a strength-building program (weight training), produced small yet measurable increases in strength, body weight and muscle mass. A reduction in the amount of body fat was also found. It is thought that these steroids act to increase the build up of muscle as well as reduce the breakdown of muscle tissue that occurs during exercise training. Another effect is their move to adverse action on the central nervous system (brain), resulting in increased aggressiveness. The positive effects of these steroids on performance are variable and are not experienced by all individuals.

© Hofoss/Rothco

While using steroids, muscle and strength development are dependent upon many factors including individual genetic make-up, the degree and history of training and personal mind state. In addition, diet, especially of protein and calorie content, plays an important role in body weight gain and amount of muscle developed. High intakes of protein, however, do not ensure that increases in muscle and strength due to steroid use will be seen.

The information available on young male and female athletes prior to or during puberty is scarce. It would be expected that these individuals would be effected more by steroid use than adults, because the female and the pre-pubescent male have lower circulating concentrations of these steroids in their blood.

Undesirable Effects

In addition to the positive effects of steroid use, many undesirable effects have also been noted. The effects of major concern are those on the liver, cardiovascular system, reproductive system and psyche.

The liver plays a central role in the breakdown of many drugs. It is possible that with a high steroid intake an overload could occur leading to liver damage. Exactly how these steroids damage the liver is unknown. Animal and human studies concur that liver structure and function can be seriously damaged by the use of high doses of steroids. Impairment of liver function may result in a clinical condition known as "jaundice." Fortunately, most of these in liver function are not fatal and most are reversible after steroid use discontinues. A serious situation related to the use of large doses of steroids is peliosis hepatitis—the development of blood-filled cysts which can rupture and lead to liver failure. Although this problem has not yet been reported in athletes, it may be occurring without their knowledge.

Liver tumors have been found in some patients who took steroids as part of their medical treatment. The majority of these tumors have been found to be non-fatal and regress after discontinued steroid use. Nevertheless, malignant tumors have been found including one fatal case in a young male bodybuilder.

Cardiovascular Disease

Cardiovascular disease appears to be the great plague of modern times, afflicting nearly 30 million people and claiming nearly a million lives each year. Although heart attacks and strokes occur suddenly, evidence indicates that they are, in reality, the result of a subtle deterioration of the circulatory system over periods of 20 to 40 or more years.

Among the risk factors for cardiovascular diseases are high blood pressure and changes in fat metabolism. Steroid use has been found in a number of cases, primarily in patients but also in athletes, to be associated with an increase in the number of risk factors for the development of cardiovascular disease. These include symptoms similar to a pre-diabetic condition, decreased blood concentrations of the "good cholesterol" (known as HDL, which is part of the body's total cholesterol), and increases in blood pressure. Additionally, animal research has shown that steroid use can lead to damage of the heart muscle itself. These problems appear to be reversible when steroid use is discontinued but represent warning signs against prolonged use.

A Risky Form of Roulette

It seems clear that athletes who use steroids are playing a risky form of roulette. The critical fact is that small doses taken for short periods is *not* the way most athletes are taking steroids. Because their effects are temporary, steroids must be in the system to be of benefit; once they are out of the system much of the strength they originally produced is lost. Here lies the problem. Athletes who make gains using steroids and hard training hate the idea of losing some of those gains, no matter how hard they may train, once they go off steroids. An additional difficulty. . . is that athletes tend to take ever larger dosages over longer periods of time. Thus the apparent increasing need of the body *for* steroids and the growing psychological dependence *on* steroids join hands to encircle the ambitious athlete.

Terry Todd, *Sports Illustrated*, August 1, 1983.

The effects of steroid use on the male reproductive system include reductions in sperm production (to the point of few viable sperm in some cases), decrease in size and tissue changes within the testes and reductions in the amount of sex hormone output, resulting in a reduced sex drive. All these changes have been observed in athletes as well as in normal healthy men and patients. These changes are reversible when steroid use has stopped, but it may be some months before things return to normal.

Females taking these steroids have been found to have reductions in female sex hormones (both estrogen and progesterone), inhibition of egg development and ovulation, and varied disruptions of the menstrual cycle. In addition, some female athletes have found that male secondary sex characteristics remain after cessation of steroid use.

Psychological Effects

In both sexes, psychological effects of steroid use include reduced or increased sexual interest and increased moodiness and aggressive behavior. Steroids are reported to cause changes in brain wave activity resembling those observed with stimulants and anti-depressants. The possibility of development of aggressive and hostile behavior should be consider prior to using steroids.

Other undesirable effects associated with steroid use include: a loss of muscular coordination (ataxia), and premature closure of the epiphysial growth plates in youths, resulting in short stature as an adult. In women this includes changes in sex characteristics such as deepening of the voice, increased oiliness of the skin, and changes in fat distribution including a reduction in breast size and changes in hair growth patterns all over the body to include beard growth, thinning of hair in the temporal region and falling out of hair in patches (alopecia). An additional finding in some male athletes and patients is the development of female breast-like tissue in response to the conversion in the body of some of these steroids to the female hormone (estrogen). These adverse reactions are believed to be dependent upon the amount of steroid used and length of time of its use. However, there is no method for predicting which individuals are more likely to develop these adverse effects, some of which are potentially hazardous. There is no reason to believe that the athlete using steroids is immune from these effects.

Unethical and Deplorable

The American College of Sports Medicine (ACSM) recognized both the need for equality and fair play in athletic competition and the link between the health of athletes and the health of both amateur and professional sports. The ACSM considers unethical the use of these steroids with the intent of gaining an athletic advantage. The College supports the position that non-steroid use is in the best interest of sport and endorses development of effective procedures for the detection of drug use and of policies that exclude from competition those athletes who refuse to abide by the rules.

Gains in body weight, muscle mass and strength have often been found to be slightly but significantly enhanced when therapeutic doses of steroids are taken in conjunction with a program of muscle-building exercise, especially by experienced athletes. A lack of information precludes definite statements on the effects of large doses and prolonged use or repeated use but medical consensus suggests adverse effects. Steroids have not been shown to increase respiratory or cardiovascular capacity or performance in endurance events.

In many clinical studies and limited research on athletes, the use of anabolic steroids has been associated with a variety of serious adverse effects on the liver, cardiovascular and reproductive systems, and psychological status. Until considerably more research is conducted, a cautious approach dictates that steroid use by athletes is potentially hazardous. Fatal complications have been observed with their use in patients.

167

In addition to our concern over the potential physical and psychological harm of steroid use, the ACSM considers the medically unjustified use of steroids as unethical and deplorable and supports fully the established traditions, rules and principles of competition as set forth by the governing bodies of the sport.

Additional copies of ACSM lay summaries can be purchased through the Public Relations Department of the American College of Sports Medicine.

Recognizing Deceptive Arguments

People who feel strongly about an issue use many techniques to persuade others to agree with them. Some of these techniques appeal to the intellect, some to the emotions. Many of them distract the reader or listener from the real issues.

Below are listed a few common examples of argumentation tactics. Most of them can be used either to advance an argument in an honest, reasonable way or to deceive or distract from the real issues. When evaluating an argument, it is important for a reader to recognize the distracting, or deceptive, appeals being used.

a. *bandwagon*—the idea that "everybody" does this or believes this

b. *scare tactics*—the threat that if you don't do this or don't believe this, something terrible will happen

c. *strawperson*—distorting or exaggerating an opponent's ideas to make one's own seem stronger

d. *personal attack*—criticizing an opponent *personally* instead of rationally debating his or her ideas

e. *testimonial*—quoting or paraphrasing an authority or celebrity to support one's own viewpoint

f. *deductive reasoning*—the idea that since a and b are true, c is also true

g. *slanters*—to persuade through inflammatory and exaggerated language instead of reason

h. *generalizations*—using statistics or facts to generalize about a population, place, or idea

169

The following activity will help to sharpen your skills in recognizing deceptive reasoning. Most of the statements below are taken from the viewpoints in this chapter. *Beside each one, mark the letter of the type of deceptive appeal being used. More than one type of tactic may be applicable. If you believe the statement is not any of the listed appeals, write N.*

1. Drug-using athletes are a corrupt and immoral lot who are disappointing the children who place such innocent faith in them.

2. Using a performance-enhancing drug to improve athletic performance is just like using caffeine to keep alert. Too much caffeine can be bad for the system just as too many performance-enhancing drugs are also bad for an athlete's system.

3. The International Olympic Committee has led the fight against drugs in sports by prohibiting "the use of any illegal or performance-enhancing drug by any athlete for any athletic competition."

4. The NFL management wants to implement drug testing, not because it's a good policy, but because they can use it to manipulate players and take all the blame for the drug problem off themselves.

5. If every coach, parent, athlete and fan stand together against drug use, we will be able to end the scourge that has threatened the sports world.

6. The anti-drug campaigners would probably label even aspirin as immoral, just to get drugs banned from sports.

7. If we do not eliminate the use of steroids in our athletic games, athletes will suffer illness and death and our traditions of fair and honorable competition will erode.

8. The results of four rookies' drug tests were leaked after they tested positive for marijuana at the NFL scouting workouts. If we can't protect the reputations of our athletes, we'd better take another look at our drug testing policies.

9. If we all support random drug testing, we may be able to help those athletes who are already on drugs and prevent those who haven't started.

Periodical Bibliography

The following articles have been selected to supplement the diverse views expressed in this chapter.

William F. Allman — "Steroids in Sports: Do They Work?" *Science 83*, November 1983.

James J. Drummey — "Cocaine Scandal Hits Baseball," *The New American*, October 7, 1985.

William Oscar Johnson — "What's Happened to Our Heroes," *Sports Illustrated*, August 15, 1983.

Jim Kaplan — "Taking Steps To Solve the Drug Dilemma," *Sports Illustrated*, May 28, 1984.

Jerry Kirshenbaum — "Back to the Dark Ages," *Sports Illustrated*, July 11, 1983.

Jamie Kitman — "The Owners' Moral Grandstanding," *The Nation*, April 26, 1986.

Jacob V. Lamar Jr. — "Scoring Off the Field," *Time*, August 25, 1986.

Robert Lipsyte — "Baseball and Drugs," *The Nation*, May 25, 1986.

Sandy Padwe — "Symptoms of a Deeper Malaise," *The Nation*, September 27, 1986.

Rick Reilly — "When the Cheers Turned to Tears," *Sports Illustrated*, July 14, 1986.

William C. Rhoden — "Today's College Athletes Face a New Sort of Test," *The New York Times*, March 29, 1987.

Barry Shapiro — "Why Spot Drug Testing Can't Work," *Sport*, January 1986.

Terry Todd — "The Steroid Predicament," *Sports Illustrated*, August 1, 1983.

Peter Ueberroth — "Inside Baseball: Drugs, Money and Expansion," *U.S. News & World Report*, October 28, 1985.

USA Today — "Opinion Debate: Steroid Abuse," January 5, 1987.

Robert O. Voy — "The Science of Fair Play," *Technology Review*, August/September 1984.

Tom Wicker — "Clean at a Price," *The New York Times*, March 21, 1987.

How Should Drugs Be Legally Prescribed?

Chapter Preface

Illegal narcotics like cocaine and heroin are bought on the street. Their quality is unregulated and their use is unsupervised; their harm is well known. Many people, however, are surprised to discover that drugs legally prescribed by a physician can be just as harmful as these illegal substances. They are even more surprised to find out that abuse of prescription drugs is a serious problem.

Some people believe that much of the abuse of prescription drugs is caused by doctors who are not careful about how they dispense medicine. Either physicians prescribe the wrong drugs, they say, or they provide drugs to patients in excessive quantities. These patients follow the dosage recommendations and become addicted without realizing it. Their doctors may not recognize the addiction either, or may not want to admit their mistake, and continue to fill the prescription.

Doctors defend themselves by pointing out that many patients do not heed the careful instructions they are given. The drugs are then ineffective and the patients ask for larger doses, unwittingly exposing themselves to the risk of addiction. Some patients, already hooked on a particular drug, obtain prescriptions from several doctors at once in order to maintain their harmful habit.

Both medical professionals and patients are becoming more aware of prescription drug abuse and are taking positive steps to eradicate the problem. Articles in popular magazines advise patients to question their doctors' prescription practices; medical journals warn physicians about malpractice suits. The debate, however, will continue as long as people disagree on the proper role of prescription drugs.

"The fact that physicians rely on chemical treatment for most . . . health problems has legitimized the overuse of drugs in our society."

Drugs Are Overprescribed

Sharon Zalewski

Sharon Zalewski is a women's health activist who has been involved in the women's health movement for several years. In 1982 she served as a consultant to the United Methodist General Board of Church and Society on women's issues. In the following viewpoint, she discusses the overprescription of drugs, especially to women and the elderly. According to Zalewski, more and more physicians are treating psychological problems with psychotropic, or mind-altering, drugs that are unnecessary and may even be harmful to the patient.

As you read, consider the following questions:

1. What does Zalewski mean by "iatrogenic junkies"?
2. According to the author, what are the five most frequently prescribed drugs?
3. What are some causes of prescription drug dependency, according to the author?

Sharon Zalewski, "Prescription Drug Addicts: Reflection of Social Ills." Reprinted with permission from *engage/social action* magazine, July/August 1985. Copyright 1985 by the General Board of Church and Society of The United Methodist Church.

Drug use has become an integral part of our society. As a result, millions of Americans have become drug dependent. Persons most often associate dependency with the use of illegal drugs or with the abuse of legal substances such as alcohol and nicotine. However, dependence is not defined by the nature or legality of the substance but by the degree that a user needs a drug to perform daily activities or utilizes a drug to induce pleasure or relief.

People who use legal drugs obtained by prescription often develop dependency in the same way as people who use illegal drugs, abuse alcohol or smoke cigarettes. Unlike other forms of dependence, addiction to prescription medication results from drug use introduced by a physician.

Prescription drug addicts are referred to as iatrogenic (doctor-caused) junkies. Iatrogenic drug dependence crosses all demographic boundaries. However, it is most prevalent among women and the elderly for a variety of social and psychological reasons.

Too Many Prescriptions

The incidence of iatrogenic drug dependency corresponds to the frequency that physicians prescribe drugs as treatment and the prevalence of highly addictive drugs among those prescriptions. According to the National Center for Health Statistics, 62 percent of office visits to private-practice physicians result in drug therapy.

Between 1980 and 1982, physicians prescribed psychotropic drugs during 69.3 million office visits; 10 percent of these prescriptions included more than one psychotropic drug. Evidence suggests that psychotropic drugs are more likely to result in dependence than other types of medication.

Psychotropic drugs include tranquilizers, antidepressants, sedatives, hypnotics, and anti-psychotic agents that affect mental and emotional states. Estimates of all prescriptions for mood-modifying medication go as high as 121 million per year.

Most Frequently Prescribed Drugs

The five most frequently prescribed psychotropic drugs are: (1) the tranquilizer Valium (diazepam), (2) the stimulant Elavil (amitriptyline), (3) the depressant Dalmane (flurazepam), (4) the tranquilizer Tranxene (clorazepate) and (5) phenobarbital, a sedative. Data from the Drug Abuse Warning Network (DAWN) of the National Institute on Drug Abuse indicate a correlation between the frequency of prescription of certain drugs and the frequency of use seen in drug-related emergency room admissions. A similar relationship exists between frequency of prescriptions and cause of drug-related deaths. It is difficult to determine whether these medical emergencies and deaths are a direct result of dependence on prescription drugs.

175

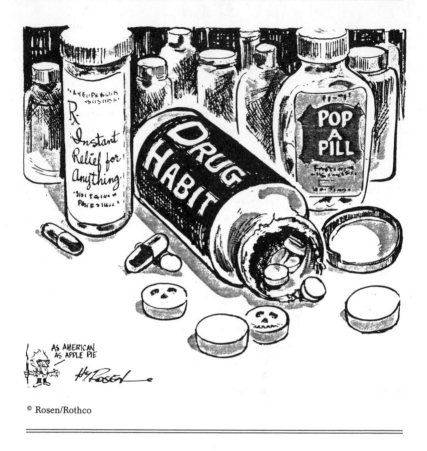

On bottle: Rx "Instant Relief for Anything"

On cylinder: DRUG HABIT

On bottle: POP A PILL

AS AMERICAN AS APPLE PIE

Trends in psychotropic drug prescription indicate that the lowest number of prescriptions go to patients under 25 while the highest number are for patients between 45 and 54. Frequency of mention of most frequently prescribed psychotropic drugs in cases of emergency room admission and deaths increases with age. For each age group, the most frequently reported cause for admission and death is alcohol in combination with another substance. This illustrates one of the most dangerous trends associated with the high levels of psychotropic drug use and alcohol use in society.

Women and Drugs

Women use legal drugs more than men. Women get twice as many prescriptions for psychotropic drugs than men. Physicians prescribe tranquilizers and sedatives twice as often for women than for men and antidepressants three times as often. Answering a survey regarding the disparity in prescription patterns, physicians cited biological vulnerability, differential stress, self-indulgence, and the reluctance of men to seek help as possible reasons.

Studies indicate that women seek help more frequently as a result of conflicts between goals and expected social roles. Drug companies, recognizing the potential market for psychotropic drugs, target women in advertising when promoting these drugs to physicians. Robert Seidenberg, a professor of psychiatry at Upstate Medical Center, State University of New York, conducted a study of drug advertisements in medical journals. He found that the ads recommended tranquilizers and anti-depressants for women distressed by boring household tasks.

In general, women are more likely to be admitted to emergency rooms for drug-related episodes than men. The most frequent drugs cited in these emergency room episodes are alcohol in combination with another substance—diazepam (Valium), aspirin, and flurazepam (Dalmane), respectively.

The most frequently cited, potentially lethal psychotropic agents in drug-related deaths are alcohol in combination with another substance and amitriptyline (Elavil). The rate at which psychotropic drugs are prescribed for women increases dramatically with age. The rate of prescription for women over 65 exceeds that of men by 60 percent.

The Elderly and Drugs

Older men and women are the largest group of legal drug users in the United States. In a limited survey conducted by the National Institute on Drug Abuse (NIDA), 62 percent of the elderly interviewed indicated that they used prescription drugs. Of these, over 33 percent reported using between two and four prescription drugs and 10 percent reported using five or more. Fifteen percent used psychotropic drugs regularly. Sixty-nine percent indicated that they also used over-the-counter drugs.

Psychotropic drug use among the elderly is also related to loneliness and lack of fulfillment. According to the NIDA survey, those persons who used psychotropic drugs indicated a need for social services that would help them establish and maintain contact with other people.

Iatrogenic drug dependence is medically caused but socially motivated. The fact that physicians rely on chemical treatment for most physical and mental health problems has legitimized the overuse of drugs in our society. Although overuse contributes to drug dependence, the social factors that cause patients to seek help in the first place cannot be ignored.

Isolation and alienation exacerbate illness and disability among the elderly. Tension caused by restrictive sex roles and social and economic inequality contributes to ill health among women.

Physicians are more likely to prescribe unnecessary psychotropic drugs for physical and mental health problems that have no pathological causes. More judicious prescription practices, particularly of psychotropic drugs, would discourage use and reduce the incidence of dependence on prescription drugs. However, drug dependence in general will not be reduced until underlying social causes are addressed.

Doing Harm

Western medicine has made a fundamental error in allowing itself to become reliant on the universal use of drug therapy.

It is an error both of philosophy and of tactics. Our examination of the effects of prescription drugs on patients, doctors and the institutions of health care has led us inevitably to this conclusion. Our statement runs counter to accepted wisdom, contradicts many popularly held beliefs and is contrary to the ideology and motivation of some of the largest and most powerful industrial interests in the world. We are convinced that the evidence is irrefutable and cannot be interpreted in any other way. We ask you to consider the possibility that drugs, rather than helping or curing, are actually doing harm.

Arabella Melville and Colin Johnson, *Cured to Death: The Effects of Prescription Drugs,* 1982.

One-third of the elderly using prescription drugs stated that they were dependent on drugs and 12 percent reported experiencing overdose and/or adverse side-effects. More persons using psychotropic drugs indicated some level of dependency. In addition, elderly users of mood-modifying drugs perceived their family relationships to be less satisfactory than non-users and indicated that their lives in general were less satisfying.

Although aging and illness are not synonymous, older people suffer more health problems than the general population. As a result their higher use of prescription medication places them at greater risk of addiction, adverse interaction between drugs, and adverse interaction between drugs and diet. These risks are compounded by a greater use of over-the-counter drugs, which cost less and are more accessible than drugs prescribed by physicians.

"Many therapists believe pharmaceuticals have a legitimate role in helping some people with psychological problems."

Drugs Are Necessary

Joseph Alper

Joseph Alper, a freelance writer, has contributed to *Science 86, The Atlantic Monthly,* and *Harpers.* In the following viewpoint, he defends the use of Valium and other psychotropic drugs. According to Alper, many therapists and other medical professionals use drugs in combination with therapy to gain the best results for their patients.

As you read, consider the following questions:

1. According to Alper, when are drugs the only effective treatment?
2. What sorts of common problems does Alper claim can be treated with drugs?
3. What kinds of drugs does the author include in his list of psychotropic drugs?

Joseph Alper, "When Drugs Work." Reprinted by permission from the June issue of SCIENCE '86. Copyright © 1986 by the American Association for the Advancement of Science.

Over the past 30 years tranquilizers, mood elevators, and sedatives have become as much a part of America's worst image as freeway traffic jams, strip mines, and burning crosses. *The Valley of the Dolls*, The Rolling Stones' song "Mother's Little Helper," and celebrity detox resorts suggest the notorious over-use of many psychotropic drugs. But despite their generally bad reputation, many therapists believe pharmaceuticals have a legitimate role in helping some people with psychological problems.

Most will agree, for example, that for severe disorders—schizophrenia, manic-depression, and extreme depression—drugs are the only effective treatment. Powerful antipsychotics such as Thorazine, the mood stabilizer lithium, and various antidepressants have revolutionized institutional psychiatry. Psychological counseling is recommended, too, but mainly to help the patients understand the need to take their medication and to cope with secondary problems that have developed as a result of being ill. People with manic-depression, for example, often are reluctant to take lithium because they miss the high-energy feeling they had while manic, despite knowing that this behavior can become destructive.

Treating Common Problems

But over the past few years, psychiatrists have found that drugs are also effective in treating more common problems. "Patients with conditions such as depression, mood swings, anxiety attacks, emotional instability, and even the underlying mood states that drive people to abuse food, drugs, or alcohol can now be helped dramatically with psychiatric medication," says psychiatrist Jacob J. Katzow, professor of psychopharmacology at George Washington University and director of the Washington, D.C., Clinic for Mood Disorders.

The most common drug used for treating psychological problems is Valium, a mild tranquilizer—or anti-anxiety drug, as researchers prefer to call it these days. (The top selling drug in 1970, Valium has dropped to fourth place during this decade.) Valium belongs to a family of compounds called benzodiazepines, which also includes Librium and Xanax, which also works as an antidepressant. Although Valium is considered one of the most widely abused substances in this country, studies have shown that it and its chemical relatives are very effective in treating what are now called generalized anxiety disorders and mild depression.

Anxiety, while a normal response to many situations that produce fearful anticipation, can be excessive. Many of its most unpleasant symptoms—insomnia, sweating, muscle tension, tension headaches, accelerated heart rate, vomiting, and shaking—can be controlled with benzodiazepines. They apparently quell activity at the brain's synapses by stimulating production of a potent natural inhibitor, gamma-aminobutyric acid.

Because psychological dependence develops with the use of all anti-anxiety drugs, therapists speak of them cautiously. Researchers at the National Institute of Mental Health are testing the effects of long-term benzodiazepine use. Pending those results, psychiatrists prescribe benzodiazepines for short periods, especially the first two months of talking therapy. According to Alan Raskin, director of the psychology division at Detroit's Lafayette Clinic, evidence "suggests that drugs can be used to reduce the anxiety level in people who come in for treatment for generalized anxiety disorder so that talking therapy can be more effective more quickly."

During the past decade, the big news in psychotropic medicines has been antidepressant drugs. Depression is the most common psychological complaint in this country: up to 20 percent of the population face at least one episode of it during their lifetimes. Only about 20 percent of these receive any treatment.

The Need for Drugs

There are people who pride themselves on "never" taking any drugs whatsoever. This is to be recommended during pregnancy, because some drugs can traverse the placenta and may cause adverse or even dangerous effects in the fetus. In all other conceivable conditions, however, not taking a drug when it might alleviate a disease or discomfort is unjustifiable. Religious fanatics may deny themselves the comfort of medications, but normal, rational individuals should never consider falling into that trap.

Alfred Burger, *Drugs and People: Medications, Their History and Origins, and the Way They Act*, 1986.

Tricyclic antidepressants are first pick in the pharmacopoeia to fight depression. Improvement is reported in about 70 percent of patients who take them. Those who do not respond to tricyclics are sometimes given another sort of antidepressant—monoamine oxidase inhibitors. Both groups of drugs alter the action and distribution of brain chemicals, but in precisely what way no one knows. It is thought that both groups prolong the life and usefulness of neurotransmitters in the brain.

There are few studies comparing the effectiveness of talking and drug therapies, although NIMH is conducting a five-year test contrasting two forms of talking therapy with drug therapy for depression. Anecdotal evidence supports the notion that combining talk and drugs works best.

Imipramine, the antidepressant prescribed most often, also appears to be effective in treating other psychological problems. Approximately 60 percent of patients with the eating disorder bulimia respond well to the drug, and studies suggest that it can also control alcoholism in some instances. And surprisingly, imipramine has now been shown to be as effective as Librium in treating generalized anxiety, according to Raskin. "How an antidepressant works to control anxiety is a mystery to us," he says. "The problem is that imipramine is sort of like a blunderbuss in that it affects numerous [chemical] systems in the brain indiscriminately."

More recently, imipramine was shown to be effective in treating agoraphobia, a debilitating fear of public places that often develops as a consequence of panic attacks. Since agoraphobia is especially resistant to both conventional talking therapies and Valium, this was considered a true breakthrough in psychiatric medicine. And new reports suggest that the benzodiazepine Xanax is also effective at controlling agoraphobia. Xanax lacks some of imipramine's side effects such as dryness of the mouth, but accumulating evidence suggests that it may foster psychological dependence.

Performance anxiety, or a fear of doing something in public, is a common phobia. Usually behavioral therapy is the treatment of choice, but some people do not respond. Neither benzodiazepines nor antidepressants work with simple phobias, but surprisingly, a class of drugs used to control high blood pressure, known as beta blockers, does. Raskin says it is not clear whether the drug is actually affecting the brain or merely controlling the queasy stomach, sweaty palms, flushing, and pounding heart that accompany the phobic reaction. Without these physical symptoms, the person about to speak before several hundred people might be able to control his fear.

A Valuable Addition

When psychiatric drugs were discovered in the 1950s, some predicted that the demise of the therapist was just a matter of time. But the compounds have not proven to be the panacea these visionaries anticipated, and their acceptance has been less than universal. In part this is because psychologists and social workers cannot prescribe drugs and are therefore less likely to see their value. Then, too, drug therapy does not always work any better than talking therapies, and many of these drugs have side effects or are addicting.

There is concern that drugs may not offer a solution to a person's problems but merely hide his symptoms. Nevertheless, the general feeling among psychiatrists is that when used with discretion, these drugs can be a valuable addition to the repertoire of psychotherapies.

"In medical school we were trained to learn and use the generic names of medications, because . . . it is much cheaper for the patient."

Generic Drugs Will Benefit the Consumer

Hugh Drummond

Hugh Drummond writes a regular column for *Mother Jones* magazine on health care issues and is a psychiatrist in a mental health clinic. In the following viewpoint, he describes the advantages of generic prescription drugs, which are becoming more popular as consumers become more cost-conscious. Drummond points out that generic drugs are required to be as good as brand names by law, and that the effort by some pharmaceutical companies to force them out of the market is just an example of capitalistic greed.

As you read, consider the following questions:

1. According to Drummond, why do most people distrust generic drugs?
2. Why, according to the author, are drug companies attacking generic drugs?
3. How would generics fit into the author's overall plan for health care in America?

Hugh Drummond, "Drugs: What's In a Name?" *Mother Jones*, April 1987. © Foundation for National Progress.

Freedom, that thing that people died for, has become in fin de siècle America the right to choose a label. When buyers become combative about *their* brand ("I'd rather fight than switch"), corporate brainwashers hail the triumph of the "consumer franchise." They work hard to get it because it sustains profits and confirms their view of themselves as virtuous and the rest of us as stupid.

Not only do all the advertisers make us believe in the sanctity of the brand name, but they play tricks on us with "generic" labels. When you buy generic toilet paper at the supermarket, thinking you're getting the same product as the brand-named one for less money, you soon learn that you are not. It's rougher and doesn't tear well at the perforations. What you're buying is economy-grade toilet paper, sometimes manufactured by the same companies, which would otherwise be marketed at economy prices even with their brand names. But this way people get the idea that buying generic means getting poorer quality, and everybody is reinforced in the belief that brand names are best.

No Difference in Generics

There is one area of market life, however, where by law there is no difference between the product with the generic label and the standard brand. The little that's left of governmental regulation assures this correlation. We're talking pharmaceuticals.

In medical school we were trained to learn and use the generic names of medications, because once the patent has run out, it is much cheaper for the patient. By the strict standards of the *U.S. Pharmacopoeia*, the purity, potency, and concentration of the medication have to be the same regardless of who manufactures it. The only permissible differences have to do with the color of the tablet or the nature of the binder holding it together: inactive ingredients such as starch, clay, or gelatin.

Once in practice, however, doctors tend to prescribe with trade names because they are simpler to remember or because of sexy drug advertisements or the smiling influence of "company representatives" who leave samples and ballpoint pens. (A pharmacist once told me that he knows exactly when a drug company "detail man" has been through the neighborhood because for several weeks the doctors write prescriptions for the trade-named drugs of that company.)

Generic Wars

Because the states spend a lot of money on drugs through Medicaid, they have tried to induce doctors to write generic rather than trade names when they prescribe. They do this by requiring the use of prescription forms that make the doctor do a little extra work, such as writing "dispense as written" or "do not substitute" if he or she insists on prescribing a trade-named preparation rather than the generic one. This threatens to cut into the profits of the drug industry, already one of the most profitable gold mines in the history of the universe.

Not surprisingly, a counterattack has begun. Advertisements, company-sponsored "symposia" with free cocktails, throwaway "journals" published by or for drug firms, and the ever-present detail men and women are crusading against generic drugs as if the trade name were the true cross. They rattle off horror stories about patients who got sick or became crazy because a switch to a generic drug resulted in a changed concentration of medication. The accompanying antigovernment and antibureaucracy rhetoric includes a dose of "don't let them tell you what to do" and a warning that socialized medicine is just around the corner. Would that it were true.

Patients Want Generics

Any redirection of prescribing or dispensing behavior from one brand of a drug to a less expensive brand of the same drug lowers the price paid by consumers. And there is ample opportunity for such savings in the prescription drug market. Approximately two-thirds of all prescriptions are for drugs with more than one brand and prices of generic substitutes are often well below those of leading brands. If told about the availability of lower-priced but generally equivalent products, patients would urge their physicians to prescribe the cheaper products or to prescribe generics.

Alison Masson and Paul H. Rubin, *Regulation*, September/October 1986.

One medical journal calling itself *Private Practice* (lest you have any illusions about its values) introduced its cover story about generics with a picture of a little girl and the words "Brand Name versus Generic: WHY TAKE A CHANCE?"

Controlled Guidelines

The good news is that for some mysterious reason the Food and Drug Administration has not yet been deregulated by the mean-spirited old man who is pushing us around in the name of free markets. The FDA has very specific and carefully controlled guidelines for generic drugs. It not only prescribes the potency and purity of the active ingredients, but considers the variety of binders and other inert substances in them, insisting that within strictly defined limits the generic drug be as bioavailable as the original one. This means that the level of active ingredients found in the blood at varying times after ingestion of the generic drug must be within 80 percent of the level of the trade-named, or pioneer, drug in 80 percent of the individuals tested.

The behemoths in the drug industry are arguing that these limits are not "safe" enough; they offer evidence based on microanalyses that equally bioavailable drugs are not "equivalent." Despite the horror stories, there is no published report of a systematic pattern of problems with substitution of generics. The carping studies offered by the companies ignore the fact that a patient's blood-level concentration is vastly more influenced by food eaten or exercise performed or other drugs taken than by substitution of a prescribed generic drug. The FDA found that while it allows a 20 percent variation in bioequivalence between generics and pioneer drugs, "the average observed difference in absorption between the two groups has been only 3.5 percent." It concluded that "there is no reason to suppose that a generic drug varies in bioequivalence from a pioneer drug any more than a subsequent formulation of a pioneer drug may vary." Furthermore, an estimated 50 percent of patients (even more of those with chronic conditions) do not take the drug as prescribed anyway.

And though you may like to think your physician has titrated the dosage of your medicine down to the precise milligram, as if each molecule of the drug were a magic bullet, the reality is that most dosage levels are prescribed within broad outlines of approximate utility.

Attacks Against Generics

The companies have not yet gone to the extent of trying to convince you, the consumer, that your doctor is irresponsible in permitting a generic to be administered. They have, however, recently begun "institutional advertisements" that urge people to ask their doctors about a company's products that might help deal with a specific health concern. (It is illegal to advertise a prescription drug by name without also noting problems associated with it.) What the industry would dearly love is a lawsuit against a doctor who prescribed a generic. Watch for it.

In the meantime, the drug companies have done something more subtle. One year before the patent ran out on Valium (the great opiate of the masses), the Roche corporation did something interesting. It redesigned the pill, replacing the undistinguished white, yellow, or blue tablets (depending on the dose) with funny discs with V-shaped holes in them that looked like ancient subway tokens. And then it trademarked the tablet's *design*.

This was not a simple aesthetic innovation. The result is that now when we prescribe a generic form of diazepam, which is pharmacologically identical to Roche's Valium, patients are inclined to say, "You gave me the wrong drug—it doesn't look the same as my blue heaven."

The McNeil company has done the same thing with Haldol, a tranquilizer taken by many psychotic patients, who might be even more sensitive to a change in the appearance of their medicine.

Ads show pictures of harried-looking folks claiming "change upsets me." There is no limit to what pharmaceutical companies will do to sustain their profits.

Nationalizing the Drug Industry

But capitalism creates a whole ecosystem of greed. It turns out that even when physicians are diligent about writing generic prescriptions, the lower costs are not always passed on to the consumer. According to one study—albeit funded by a drug company and published in the *Journal of the American Medical Association*—pharmacies mark up generic drugs at a higher rate than brand ones, which means higher profits for them and only minimal savings, if any, for the consumer.

Big Companies' Smear Campaign

This "smear and fear" campaign against generic drugs is of particular concern . . . because it is victimizing millions of older persons. They are the primary users of long-term maintenance drugs for chronic conditions and could save a great deal of money by using generics. Yet they are being scared away from generics by those who impugn their safety and efficacy for purely economic reasons.

Cyril F. Brickfield, address at the Conference on Pharmaceuticals for the Elderly, Washington, DC, February 13, 1986.

The conclusion of all this is obvious: the manufacture and distribution of medicine should not be a matter of private profit. The nationalization of the drug industry will have to be part of any sensible government health program. As long as medication remains such an important part of health care, there is no point in talking about socialized medicine without socializing *medicine.*

"The real cost of generic drugs [will be] . . . a reduction in the quality of research and development at the frontiers of biomedical science."

Generic Drugs Will Ultimately Harm the Consumer

Roger P. Maickel

Roger P. Maickel is a professor in the Department of Pharmacology and Toxicology in the School of Pharmacy and Pharmacal Sciences at Purdue University. He is also a scientific advisor to the American Council on Science and Health in New York. In the following viewpoint, he contends that generic drugs are not the bargains they appear to be, because they shift revenue away from the pharmaceutical companies that are doing vital and costly research on new drugs. The loss of such research will mean a loss to the consumer.

As you read, consider the following questions:

1. According to Maickel, how were drugs dispensed until the 1950s?
2. What, according to the author, is one of the primary costs of developing a new drug? How do generics avoid this cost?
3. Why does the author think that generic drugs will harm the pharmaceutical industry in the long run?

Roger P. Maickel, "The Real Cost of Generic Drugs," *ACSH News & Views*, May/June 1985. Reprinted with permission.

The U.S. consumer has been inundated by a "new" concept in marketing—"generic" products. Such products are often packaged in black-and-white or other non-unique and sometimes nondescript containers, generally devoid of any brand/manufacturer's name. The retail price is somewhat lower than the regular retail prices of branded competitors, and the quality of any given product may be equal to or less than that of its brand name competitors, based on comparative evaluation testing. The public, in general, feels that generic products offer a maximal saving in costs with a minimal reduction in quality. As a result, we now have generic canned foods, generic paper products, generic soda pop, generic beer, generic cigarettes, generic aspirin, and generic prescription drugs.

It's clear that generic products offer consumers substantial savings. But do they provide comparable quality? And do they have hidden costs? In the case of generic prescription drugs, the answer to one of these questions is reassuring, but the other may give us cause for concern.

The History of Generic Drugs

The concept of generic, (i.e., non-brand name) pharmaceutical products is not really new. Until the upsurge of prepackaged prescription drugs in the 1950s, many medicines were prepared by mixing bulk ingredients in the individual neighborhood pharmacy. While the component ingredients (active drugs, binders, solvents, flavors, etc.) were purchased by the pharmacist from manufacturers, the actual product delivered to the customer was produced in its final form (compounded) by Mr. Smith—the pharmacist. The ingredients had to meet the standards of the United States Pharmacopeia; the final products were theoretically similar from pharmacy to pharmacy but certainly were not as uniform as the standardized products of a modern industrial production line. Some idea of the state of the pharmaceutical industry in the United States less than 50 years ago may be seen in the fact that in 1940 not one manufacturer of ethical (prescription) drugs in this country had an annual sales volume larger than that of Macy's department store in New York City.

The onset of World War II brought a shift in the leadership of the pharmaceutical industry from Europe to the United States with a concurrent increase in research and development. The impetus of military problems stimulated research to develop new and better vaccines and drugs; the use of these agents in battlefield situations demanded new and better dosage forms and drug delivery systems. The concept of prepackaged, pre-measured, easily stored and readily dispensed dosage systems was stimulated, and by the late 1940s the days of the compounding pharmacist were rapidly nearing an end.

As pharmaceutical companies became the manufacturers of the final products used, their need to extend their efforts into new drug development became more pronounced; at the same time, scientists around the world began to develop newer approaches to the therapy of human diseases. A host of new drugs—many in therapeutic classes previously unknown—were born. For example, since 1945 (only four decades ago), we have seen the development of antibiotics, tranquilizers, oral contraceptives and many others.

Developing a New Drug

Developing a new therapeutic agent is much like trying to breed pandas in captivity—a lengthy and expensive process with a very low probability of success. Of every 1,000 chemical compounds prepared by a pharmaceutical company—either isolated from a natural source or synthesized in the chemical laboratory—*one* or *two* will actually develop into marketable drugs. From the date a substance is first isolated or synthesized in sufficient quantities for the start of testing to when the compound is actually sold in the marketplace, six to eight years generally elapse, and the cost may be anywhere from 25 to 75 million dollars.

A Caution About Generic Drugs

Although generics meet U.S. Food and Drug Administration standards and are tested for their equivalence to the brand name product—that is, they have the same *active* ingredients—they may have different *inactive* ingredients. Changing from the brand name to the generic, or between different generics, may make a difference if you're used to one particular product.

Valerie DeBenedette, *Health*, April 1986.

At some point during the process of drug development, often rather early, the manufacturer files a patent application. From the date of issuance of the patent, the manufacturer has a period of 17 years of sole rights to sell the drug. After that, competitors who wish to market the drug as a generic can enter the picture. But it's important to remember that new drugs are usually patented long before the date when they are actually approved for sale by the Food and Drug Administration (FDA). Thus, the actual opportunity for the company to regain the cost of development (and some of the cost of the aborted development of other drugs that fell by the wayside during the long development process) without market competition may be as little as five to seven years. Until very recently, it might have been even shorter if the red tape of the FDA's review process for new drugs became more than usually

190

tangled, thus delaying the drug's final approval.

Two decades of controversy over generic drugs culminated in the passage of the Drug Price Competition and Patent Term Restoration Act of 1984, signed into law by President Reagan on September 24, 1984.

Problems with Drug Development

The controversy had focused on two issues, and the new law deals with both of them. One key concern was the decreasing incentive for manufacturers to develop new drugs, caused by the shortened patent protection produced by stringent regulatory requirements and lengthy approval processes. The other problem was the difficulty that manufacturers of generic drugs were having in getting their products approved by FDA, because of complex regulatory procedures.

The new law covers a variety of aspects of drug patenting and development. Indeed, most experts are of the opinion that various types of legal situations will require extensive litigations and court tests to fully define the "new" procedures. In general terms, however, the law accomplishes the following two things.

First, numerous parts of the new law concern extension of patent terms to allow for delays in review and/or approval of truly new drugs by the FDA. Such extensions may not exceed five years *per se*, nor may the time from the date of the drug's approval to the termination of the patent extension exceed 14 years.

Second, the new law establishes specific procedures which should facilitate the approval of generic versions after a drug's patent expires.

Despite the extension of patent protection which it provides, the new law's overall impact is expected to be an increase in the availability of generic drugs. This should reduce the overall cost of health care in the United States by stimulating price competition for prescription pharmaceuticals. What are some of the implications of this for the consumer?

Implications of Generic Drugs

There is no question that a generic version of a drug can be sold for a lower price than the original version of the same drug, since the overall cost of development of the generic is considerably smaller. Unlike the developer of the truly new (pioneer) drug, the developer of the generic need not conduct research to prove that the drug is safe and effective. He need only prove that his product has bioavailability and bioequivalency comparable to the original (i.e., that it gets to its destination in the body as efficiently as the original drug does, and that it acts as effectively once it arrives). The research required to demonstrate bioavailability and bioequivalency is minimal in comparison with the research required to develop a pioneer drug.

Because bioavailability and bioequivalency must be demonstrated before a generic version of a drug is marketed, the generic drug is therapeutically the same as the pioneer product. Therefore, consumers who take advantage of the generic's lower cost do not have to sacrifice therapeutic effectiveness to do so. FDA regulations ensure that they do not have to sacrifice quality either. All manufacturers of prescription pharmaceuticals are required to maintain similar standards of quality by the FDA. Thus, all must follow the requirements of Good Manufacturing Practices and must exist within similar constraints for quality control. While it may be tempting to cut corners in manufacturing procedures, any decrease in quality will lead to FDA- or manufacturer-initiated recalls with consequent financial losses to the manufacturer.

The Real Cost of Generic Drugs

What then are the concerns, if any, that need be expressed regarding the expected influx of generic prescription drugs into the marketplace? One major concern stands out. At the present time, the manufacturers of pioneer drugs return a significant portion of their profits on marketed drugs to their in-house research efforts; much of this funding goes to support basic research into the causes of disease as well as into the development of completely new therapeutic approaches. The generic manufacturers have, in general, no such in-house research capabilities. As a result, one might very well expect to see fewer and fewer truly new drugs being developed in this country.

While generic versions of a drug rarely achieve the lion's share of a market, a significant decrease in market share held by a pioneer manufacturer, coupled with a competition-induced selling price reduction, will lead to a reduction in company-available research and development funding. In the long run, this will be the real cost of generic drugs, not a saving in dollars but a reduction in the quality of research and development at the frontiers of biomedical science.

Unless a manufacturer can foresee the rewards of an active research program and can return those rewards to furthering development, the pharmaceutical industry in the U.S. may face a future that is characterized by a high degree of competition for lower prices rather than for new and better products. The tremendous improvements in pharmacotherapeutics (use of drugs in the treatment of diseases) since the end of World War II have emanated largely from research efforts of the "pioneer drug" pharmaceutical industry; one must hope that the rise of generic drugs will not lead to a reversal of this trend.

"The evidence that marijuana has medical value is overwhelming."

Marijuana Should Be Used for Medicinal Purposes

Kevin B. Zeese

Kevin B. Zeese was the national director for NORML, the National Organization for the Reform of Marijuana Laws. He continues to administer NORML's legal program while practicing law in Alexandria, Virginia. In the following viewpoint, he explains why NORML has fought for legalization of marijuana as a medicine. According to Zeese, marijuana can be an effective way of treating many illnesses.

As you read, consider the following questions:

1. What are some uses for marijuana as a medicine, according to Zeese?
2. What irony does the author see in the present laws prohibiting marijuana?
3. According to the author, what evidence exists that marijuana has an accepted medical use in the United States?

Kevin B. Zeese, "Recreational Marijuana Should Not Prevent Medical Marijuana," from *High Times*, December 1986. © 1986 by Trans-High Corporation.

One of the saddest things about the debate over whether marijuana should be legalized is that it has gotten tangled up with the question of whether someone should be allowed to use marijuana as a medicine.

Marijuana could be a helpful medicine in preventing the blindness of glaucoma, the muscle spasticity of various illnesses, the nausea caused by cancer therapies and a host of other serious medical illnesses. Even though thousands of Americans, perhaps even one to two million, need marijuana for medical purposes, it is virtually impossible to get marijuana legally. Seriously ill Americans are suffering because of the "sins" of the tens of millions of Americans who consume marijuana for relaxation and recreation.

NORML has been trying to change that. In 1972 we filed a petition with the Bureau of Narcotics and Dangerous Drugs [BNDD], the forerunner of the DEA [Drug Enforcement Administration], to have marijuana rescheduled under the federal Controlled Substances Act. Currently marijuana is classified as a Schedule I drug. This schedule is the most restrictive. It is for substances which have no medical value. It is the schedule for "hated" drugs like heroin and LSD. As a result of being placed in Schedule I, marijuana is not available for medical use, and it is very difficult to even conduct research on marijuana.

The Need for Marijuana

The bureaucrats who enforce the drug laws have fought the NORML petition every step of the way. NORML has filed lawsuits six times over the 15 years of our petition. Each suit was an attempt to get the government to look at the facts. Over the life of our suit countless Americans have suffered, and even died, because of the lack of medicinal marijuana. It is sad and ironic that no recreational marijuana user has ever died, but that people who need marijuana as medicine are suffering serious life-threatening and sense-threatening illnesses.

Three of our lawsuits have resulted in decisions by the U.S. Court of Appeals for the District of Columbia. Each time the court has ruled in NORML's favor and each time the court has expressed concerns about the way the drug enforcement bureaucrats were handling NORML's petition.

After the first denial of the petition in 1974, the Court of Appeals described the action of the BNDD as "not the kind of agency action that promoted the kind of interchange and refinement of views that is the lifeblood of a sound administrative process." Those are harsh words from a court, but they are mild when it is realized that the BNDD rejected NORML's petition **out of hand** *without* taking any testimony or other evidence.

The DEA rejected NORML's petition again in 1977. This time

the Court of Appeals was critical because the DEA had failed to obtain scientific and medical evaluations of marijuana from the federal health agencies. The court properly pointed out that this scientific review was specifically required by the Controlled Substances Act.

More Information

The third decision by the Court of Appeals came in 1980 after NORML's petition was again rejected. This time the court specifically ordered the DEA to obtain health information on marijuana and ended its order saying: "We regrettably find it necessary to remind respondents (the DEA) of an agency's obligation on remand not to do anything which is contrary to either the letter or spirit of the mandate" of this court.

Since 1980 the Court of Appeals has found it necessary to spur the bureaucrats along further by requiring the DEA and the department of Health and Human Services to file quarterly reports with the court on progress in reviewing the NORML petition. This came after successive court filings by NORML in 1981 and 1982.

Better Than Other Drugs

In the past it has been argued that, while marijuana may have some useful effects, it is not needed because other drugs do the same things better and without the cannabis side effects. The latest findings, however, indicate situations in which cannabis may be better than other available drugs. Dr. Louis Vachon of Boston University said that THC "has a remarkably low toxicity in laboratory animals and human beings." When compared to other powerful medications now in use, he noted, "it shows a strikingly low lethality and very little respiratory-depressant activity."

Jules Saltman, *Marijuana: Current Perspectives*, 1976.

Non-lawyers reading this may ask "why hasn't the court just overruled the DEA and rescheduled marijuana to allow its medical use?" That would be a highly unusual action for a court. Courts generally defer to the government agencies as they are "the experts." They deal with marijuana, medicine and related issues on a daily basis. Especially in this case where there has been no record developed on which the court can make its own findings of fact.

However, finally after 15 years of litigation, there is hope for progress on the medical marijuana issue. As a result of negotiations between NORML and the DEA, the DEA has scheduled hearings before an administrative law judge. For the first time, the question of marijuana's medical value will be heard before an impartial arbitrator. This will give NORML an opportunity to build a strong record which the Court of Appeals can act on.

Why has the DEA avoided and delayed a hearing on the merits of NORML's petition for so many years? Because the evidence that marijuana has medical value is overwhelming and the DEA does not want to admit anything good about marijuana. They think that doing so would undercut all of marijuana policy and that Americans are not intelligent enough to differentiate between medical use and non-medical use.

In a book published [in 1986] *Cannaboids as Therapeutic Agents* (CRC Press, Inc., 2000 Corporate Blvd., Boca Raton, Florida, 33431), Raphel Mechoulam, an Israeli who was the first to separate THC from marijuana, reviews all of the research on the medical value of marijuana and its component parts. He begins by reviewing the history of marijuana in medicine. He looks at the ancient Middle East and Europe, the Middle Ages, India, Persia, China, and western Europe and North America in the 19th and 20th centuries.

Mechoulam finds marijuana has been used in medicine *"for millenia."* He lists twenty broad areas where marijuana has been used in history and notes that ten of these medicinal uses have been proven correct by research in the last two decades. The ten medicinal uses confirmed by recent research include its use as an analgetic (painkiller), an antiasthmatic, an anticonvulsive, a sedative, a hypnotic, an antirheumatic, an antidiarrheal, an antibiotic, an appetite promoter and an antipyretic (fever reducer).

The book goes on to review the major areas where research on cannabis and medicine have occurred. These include treatment of neurological disorders, effects on the eyes primarily for treatment of glaucoma, as an anti-nausea agent in cancer therapy and as a bronchodilator.

Accepted Medical Use

Not only is there strong evidence in history and current research showing the medical value of marijuana, but there are other indications that marijuana has an accepted medical use in the United States. Thirty-three states have passed laws recognizing and authorizing marijuana as a medicine. (Unfortunately, these states need to get their marijuana from the federal government, so very few have active programs.) In addition, courts have recognized the medical value of marijuana in cases where individuals were prosecuted on marijuana charges and claimed they needed marijuana as a medicine.

Even the DEA has recognized the medical value of marijuana's major psychoactive ingredient, THC. Earlier this year the DEA rescheduled a synthetic THC pill to be used in treating nausea caused by cancer chemotherapy. The pill is being marketed under the brand name Marinol.

The DEA's acknowledgment of THC's medical value puts them in an indefensible position. There have been studies conducted in five states comparing THC pills with marijuana cigarettes. Each study has found that marijuana was much more effective than THC and that it was also safer. Thus, due to the debate over marijuana policy generally, the DEA has approved a less effective, more dangerous drug for medical use. The senselessness of their decision will be obvious when the hearings on NORML's petition are completed.

"There is no pharmacological or medical justification for the use of marijuana."

Marijuana Is Not Effective as a Medicine

Gabriel G. Nahas

Gabriel G. Nahas is a pharmacologist, educator, and author who has lectured and conducted seminars all over the world. He is professor of anesthesiology at the College of Physicians and Surgeons of Columbia University, adjunct professor at the University of Paris, and consultant to the United Nations Commission on narcotics. In the following viewpoint, excerpted from his book, *Keep Off the Grass*, Nahas refutes claims that marijuana can be used as a medicine. Even when pure THC, the active ingredient in marijuana, is used, he says, it is not as effective as other drugs.

As you read, consider the following questions:

1. In what way is the public confused about marijuana's medicinal value, according to Nahas?
2. To what does Nahas compare a dose of marijuana? Why does he make this comparison?
3. According to the author, what characteristics of marijuana limit its use as a medicine?

Gabriel G. Nahas, *Keep Off the Grass*. Middlebury, VT: Paul S. Eriksson, Publisher, 1985. Reprinted with permission.

Marijuana as medicine regained popularity and favor in the wake of the widespread use of marijuana as an intoxicant in the United States during the second part of the twentieth century.

To the old claims, new applications widely heralded by the medical and lay press were found for the old drug, in the treatment of glaucoma and of nausea and vomiting induced by cancer chemotherapy.

A powerful lobby, the Alliance for Cannabis Therapeutics, having close ties with NORML, the National Organization for the Reform of Marijuana Laws was formed in Washington, D.C. Its stated purpose was to "end the federal prohibition of cannabis in medicine and construct a medically meaningful, ethically correct and compassionate system of regulation which permits the seriously ill to legally obtain cannabis." This lobby was able to form an alliance of patients and their families, concerned citizens, humanitarians, public officials and elected officials.

Public Confusion

In response to such political and public pressure, twenty-four states passed legislation which authorized the prescription of cannabis crude-drug preparations for the management of nausea and vomiting related to cancer chemotherapy. A bill (H.R. 4498) was presented in the U.S. Congress "to provide for the therapeutic use of marijuana in situations involving life-threatening or sense-threatening illness and to provide supplies of marijuana for such use."

It would appear that some confusion has permeated the mind of the public, and of its representatives, who are not aware of the therapeutic revolution of the thirties and fail to distinguish between a crude drug and its pharmacologically active pure components, in this instance, too many have failed to distinguish between marijuana and THC.

Marijuana vs. THC

Dr. Carlton Turner pointed out that while crude-cannabis preparations containing delta-9-THC display similar pharmacological properties as their main psychoactive compound, their overall effect is different. The other cannabinoids . . . present in the crude material interact with the absorption, availability and transformation of delta-9-THC in the body. The other chemicals contained in the plant material . . . also possess some specific biological activity. Furthermore, the respective amounts of chemicals contained in each preparation will vary over a wide range: no two samples of crude marijuana, drawn from two different batches of plants, will have the same composition: they are therefore two different drugs, and this holds true for their THC content. Marijuana, the crude drug obtained from a single can-

199

nabis plant harvested at 8:00 A.M. will be different from the marijuana obtained from the *same plant* harvested at 10:00 A.M. on the same day. When the crude drug is smoked, it contains toxic substances such as benzopyrene, a cancer-causing chemical produced by the burning process: it is 70% more abundant in marijuana smoke than in tobacco smoke. Crude-drug marijuana . . . used for smoking in the United States can also be contaminated with salmonella bacteria which gives diarrhea, and with a fungus aspergillus, which may cause severe bronchopneumonia. . . . It would be practically impossible for a crude drug like marijuana therefore to comply with the Pure Food and Drug Act which requires that all medicines be labelled with the exact amount of chemicals they contain. . . .

An Unstable Substance

Marijuana is an unstable substance. It has a poor shelf life. It will be found to contain over a thousand chemicals—we only know of about four hundred-odd now but that's because we haven't been researching it very long—and it contains dozens of things that may not contribute to what we want it to do.

Sidney Cohen, *Marijuana Alert*, 1985.

There is no pharmacological or medical justification for the use of marijuana, the crude drug, in the treatment of specific ailments. Such use may be compared to the administration of a cocktail of unknown composition with resulting unpredictable effects—akin to the practice of voodoo medicine. Most of the therapeutic applications attributed to cannabis the crude drug have been traced down to the effect of its main psychoactive ingredient delta-9-THC and to a lesser extent to the nonpsychoactive cannabidol.

Many of the medical indications suggested for THC—against pain, convulsions, depression, anxiety, asthma, as a sedative and hypnotic and a tranquillizer—did not go beyond self-limiting clinical trials. However, two new indications were found: to treat the vomiting associated with cancer chemotherapy and glaucoma. Dr. Richard Gralla from the Sloane Kettering Cancer Institute of New York reported at Oxford a study which compared THC and metoclopramide in the treatment of nausea and vomiting induced by cisplatin. Cisplatin is a powerful anti-cancer drug which causes a great deal of vomiting. Gralla concluded that THC was less effective in controlling vomiting than metoclopramide administered in high dose by the intravenous route. I reported in turn that at Columbia Presbyterian Hospital in New York metoclopramide was the drug of choice to prevent vomiting in cancer chemotherapy; and, recent studies carried out in collaboration with Dr. Henri Roche and Dr. George Hyman indicated that an old drug, compazine, when given intravenously, was more effective than metoclopramide.

Drawbacks to THC

The use of THC in the treatment of glaucoma was reported by Dr. John Merritt of Chapel Hill University, North Carolina. The lack of a THC preparation which could be applied directly on the eye, and the hypertension and the side effects of THC administered orally, or smoked, limited the clinical trials of this drug. Louis Lemberger of Indianapolis reported the clinical use of a synthetic derivative of THC, Nabilone, to control vomiting in patients receiving cancer chemotherapy. Nabilone is now available for this purpose in the United States. Its effectiveness and incidence of side effects must still be compared with those of compazine and metoclopramide which do remain the drugs of choice associated with corticosteroids.

Dr. J. Trounce, from Guy's Hospital in London, . . . concluded with a typical British understatement: "Unless a new and more scientific indication for cannabis and its derivatives emerges or it is possible by modifying its structure to isolate one of its potentially useful pharmacological actions, it seems unlikely that this group of drugs will play a major role in therapeutics."

The reasons for the clinical lack of success of THC as medicine in the 20th century are the same as those encountered by the physicians of the 19th century who attempted to use cannabis extracts for a wide variety of ailments. These reasons inherent in the drug are: the diversity and variability of its actions, its limited and inconsistent absorption into the body and its undesirable side effects.

Understanding Words in Context

Readers occasionally come across words which they do not recognize. And frequently, because they do not know a word or words, they will not fully understand the passage being read. Obviously, the reader can look up an unfamiliar word in a dictionary. However, by carefully examining the word in the context in which it is used, the word's meaning can often be determined. A careful reader may find clues to the meaning of the word in surrounding words, ideas, and attitudes.

Below are excerpts from the viewpoints in this chapter. In each excerpt, one or two words are printed in italics. Try to determine the meaning of each word by reading the excerpt. Under each excerpt you will find four definitions for the italicized word. Choose the one that is closest to your understanding of the word.

Finally, use a dictionary to see how well you have understood the words in context. It will be helpful to discuss with others the clues which helped you decide on each word's meaning.

1. Drug use has become an *INTEGRAL* part of our society. As a result, millions of Americans have become drug dependent.

   INTEGRAL means:

   a) kind   ✓c) essential
   b) laughable   d) forgotten

2. Dependence on prescription drugs crosses all *DEMOGRAPHIC* boundaries. However, it is most prevalent among women and the elderly.

   DEMOGRAPHIC means:

   a) population   c) key
   b) red   d) written

3. It would appear that confusion has *PERMEATED* the mind of the public. No one is able to distinguish between marijuana, a harmful drug, and pure THC, its helpful primary ingredient.

PERMEATED means:

a) drugged   c) filled
b) announced   d) emptied

4. They're lonely, they can't get to the doctor, and they often forget to take their medicine. These factors *EXACERBATE* illness among the elderly.

EXACERBATE means:

✓a) make worse   c) stretch
b) remove   d) bring together

5. The level of medication found in a patient's blood after *INGESTION* of the tablet or capsule must be within certain limits.

INGESTION means:

a) swallowing   ✓c) indigestion
b) breaking   d) marketing

6. When psychiatric drugs began eliminating the need for psychiatric counseling, some predicted the *DEMISE* of the therapist was just a matter of time.

DEMISE means:

a) home   c) cheerfulness
✓b) end   d) rank

7. Though you may like to think your physician has *TITRATED* the dosage of your medicine down to the precise milligram, most doses are prescribed within broad outlines.

TITRATED means:

a) forced   c) hampered
b) thrown   d) measured

8. There is a *CORRELATION* between the drugs that physicians safely prescribe in their offices and the drugs found in patients who are brought to the emergency room because of an overdose.

CORRELATION means:

✓a) connection   c) charge
b) need   d) forgetfulness

Periodical Bibliography

The following articles have been selected to supplement the diverse views expressed in this chapter.

Stefan Bechtel — "Medicinal Drugs That Can Make You an Addict," *Prevention*, February 1984.

Anthony Brandt — "Out of Control," *Esquire*, April 1984.

Cyril F. Brickfield — "Pharmaceutical Industry and the Consumer," *Vital Speeches of the Day*, April 15, 1986.

Rebecca Coffey — "Drugged Driving," *Science Digest*, September 1986.

Consumers' Research Magazine — "Prescription Drug Abuse," January 1983.

Allan Dodds Frank — "Dear Pharmacist," *Forbes*, June 16, 1986.

Lindsay Van Gelder — "Dependencies of Independent Women," *Ms.*, February 1987.

Dale H. Gieringer — "Compassion vs. Control: FDA Investigational-Drug Regulation," *USA Today*, March 1987.

Paul Lavrakas — "Generic Drugs: What's in a Name?" *Consumers' Research Magazine*, January 1986.

Roger W. Miller — "Would RX Ads Make People Learn or Yearn?" *FDA Consumer*, October 1983.

Ms. — "Patterns of Addiction," February 1987.

Alan L. Otten — "Some States Monitor Prescriptions To Curb Abuse of Addictive Drugs," *The Wall Street Journal*, August 16, 1985.

Robert Rodale — "Saving Yourself from More Sickness," *Prevention*, April 1983.

Ellen Switzer — "Overmedication: Health Hazard of Our Time," *Vogue*, March 1986.

Organizations To Contact

The editors have compiled the following list of organizations which are concerned with the issues debated in this book. All of them have publications available for interested readers. The descriptions are derived from materials provided by the organizations themselves.

American Civil Liberties Union (ACLU)
132 W. 43rd St.
New York, NY 10036
(212) 944-9800

The ACLU champions the rights set forth in the Declaration of Independence and the Constitution. The Union opposes indiscriminate urine testing as a violation of the right to privacy. It publishes *Drug Testing in the Workplace* and numerous other brochures on drug use and civil liberties.

American College of Sports Medicine (ACSM)
PO Box 1440
Indianapolis, IN 46206
(317) 637-9200

The College is a research and educational organization concerned with health and sports. The College considers it unethical to use steroids or other performance enhancing drugs for athletic competition. It publishes position papers for $1.75 and lay summaries of those position papers for $1.00.

American Council for Drug Education (ACDE)
5820 Hubbard Dr.
Rockville, MD 20852
(301) 984-5700

The Council strives to educate the American public about the health hazards associated with the use of marijuana and other psychoactive substances. It believes that an informed public is the nation's best defense against drug abuse. It publishes *The Drug Educator*, quarterly, along with many pamphlets and books on drug abuse.

Committees of Correspondence
57 Conant St., Room 113
Danvers, MA 01923
(617) 774-2641

Committees of Correspondence is a national citizens' group that exchanges information on drug abuse issues in an effort to stop the drug abuse epidemic. It strongly supports anti-drug policies. Its publications include a monthly *Drug Abuse Newsletter* and several pamphlets.

Do It Now Foundation
PO Box 5115
Phoenix, AZ 85010
(602) 257-0797

The Foundation was created by people who are concerned about amphetamine use in Los Angeles. It warns young people about the dangers of drug use by public service announcements featuring rock music personalities. It publishes *Newservice*, bimonthly.

Drugs Anonymous
PO Box 473, Ansonia Station
New York, NY 10023

Drugs Anonymous' purpose is to apply the same approach as Alcoholics Anonymous to persons dependent on addictive drugs. It provides emotional support to its members and teaches methods of coping with pain that do not require drugs. It publishes numerous pamphlets on treatments for drug abuse.

Drug Enforcement Administration (DEA)
1405 I St., NW
Washington, DC 20537
(202) 633-1000

The Drug Enforcement Administration is charged with enforcing narcotics and controlled substance laws. This agency concentrates on stopping high-level narcotics smuggling and distribution organization in the United States and abroad. It publishes *Drug Enforcement Magazine*.

Families in Action
3845 N. Druid Hills Road, Suite 300
Decatur, GA 30033
(404) 325-5799

Families in Action was the nation's first community-based parent group formed to prevent drug abuse among children. It has proposed bills to ban the sale of drug paraphernalia. It publishes *Drug Abuse Update*.

Hazelden Foundation
Box 11
Center City, MN 55012
(612) 257-4010

The Foundation provides comprehensive treatment and rehabilitation for chemically dependent persons. It publishes *Newsletter* quarterly, *Professional Update*, quarterly, and a catalog of educational materials.

International Commission for the Prevention of Alcoholism and Drug Dependency (ICPADD)
6830 Laurel St., NW
Washington, DC 20012
(202) 722-6729

The Commission is an organization of scientific, political, and religious leaders who study drug dependency and its effects on society. The Commission's goal is to prevent drug abuse. It publishes a quarterly *Bulletin*.

Libertarian Party
301 W. 21st St.
Houston, TX 77008
(713) 880-1776

The Libertarian Party's goal is to ensure the respect for individual rights as the precondition for a free and prosperous world. It advocates the repeal of all laws prohibiting the production, sale, possession, or use of drugs. It publishes *Libertarian Party News* and many books.

Narcotics Anonymous (NA)
PO Box 9999
Van Nuys, CA 91409
(818) 780-3951

Narcotics Anonymous is an organization of recovering addicts who offer help to others recovering from drug addiction. It believes that for addicts to recover, they must abstain from all mood-altering drugs. Its publications include a monthly, *N.A. Way,* a book, *The Narcotics Anonymous Basic Test,* and many pamphlets.

Narcotics Education, Inc.
6830 Laurel St., NW
Washington, DC 20012
(202) 722-6740

Narcotics Education develops and distributes teaching aids for drug education and prevention. It publishes a catalog free of charge and offers other materials for a fee.

National Association of Drug Abuse Problems (NADAP)
355 Lexington Ave.
New York, NY 10017
(212) 986-1170

The Association believes the fight against drug and substance abuse will only be won by further knowledge and education. The primary focus of the group is to rehabilitate former drug users and provide opportunities for them to re-enter the work force. It publishes *Recent Developments Memo,* monthly, and *Report,* quarterly.

National Association of State Alcohol and Drug Abuse Directors (NASADAD)
444 N. Capitol St., NW, Suite 530
Washington, DC 20001
(202) 783-6868

The Association coordinates comprehensive drug abuse education and prevention programs in every state. It publishes *Monthly Report* and *Special Report.*

National Clearinghouse for Alcohol and Drug Information
PO Box 2345
Rockville, MD 20852
(301) 443-6487

The Clearinghouse is the educational arm of the National Institute on Drug Abuse. It publishes information, including several pamphlets, to increase knowledge and promote effective strategies to deal with drug abuse.

National Drug Institute
112 Sladen St.
Dracut, MA 01826
(617) 957-4442

The Institute provides consultation and training to private industries, school systems, health care professionals, and others in the area of substance abuse prevention and education. It also provides reprints of articles on these topics.

National Federation of Parents for Drug-Free Youth (NFP)
8730 Georgia Ave., Suite 200
Silver Spring, MD 20910
(301) 585-5437

The Federation believes that illegal drugs are a destructive force in society and that parents can stop drug abuse among youth. It assists in the formation of local parent groups in communities across the United States. It publishes a quarterly *Newsletter, Parent Group Starter Kit, Press/Media Guidelines,* and *Anti-Paraphernalia Kit.*

National Organization for the Reform of Marijuana Laws (NORML)
2001 S St., NW, #640
Washington, DC 20009
(202) 332-9110

NORML seeks to end all criminal penalties for personal possession, use, and cultivation of marijuana. Its publications include *Leaflet* and *Commonsense*, both quarterly, and numerous brochures.

National Parent Resource Institute for Drug Education (PRIDE)
100 Edgewood Ave., Suite 1216
Atlanta, GA 30303
(800) 241-7946

The Institute is committed to providing the most up-to-date information on drug abuse, its causes, and prevention. It organizes local parent groups to combat drug abuse through education. Its publications include a quarterly *Newsletter* and *Drug Conference Proceedings*.

Phoenix House
164 W. 74th St.
New York, NY 10023
(212) 595-5810

The House provides drug abuse treatment through individual, group, and family counseling and vocational rehabilitation. It publishes *Newsletter*, three times a year and *Journal*, annually.

Wisconsin Clearinghouse
1245 East Washington Ave.
Madison, WI 53703
(608) 236-2797

The Clearinghouse is an educational resource with information about preventing drug and alcohol abuse. It publishes a bibliography and articles related to drug and alcohol abuse prevention.

Bibliography of Books

James B. Bakalar and Lester Grinspoon
Drug Control in a Free Society. New York: Cambridge University Press, 1984.

Eve Bargmann, Sidney M. Wolfe, Joan Levin and the Public Citizen Health Research Group
Stopping Valium. Washington, DC: Public Citizen Health Research Group, Inc., 1982.

Margaret Blasingsky and George K. Russell, eds.
Urine Testing for Marijuana Use: Implications for a Variety of Settings. Rockville, MD: American Council for Drug Education, 1981.

Sidney Cohen and Therese Andrysiak
The Therapeutic Potential of Marijuana's Components. Rockville, MD: American Council for Drug Education, 1982.

Bob Goldman, with Patricia Bush and Ronald Katz
Death in the Locker Room: Steroids and Sports. South Bend, IN: Icarus Press, 1984.

Erich Goode
Drugs in American Society. Westminster, MD: Random House Publishers, 1984.

Richard A. Hawley
The Purposes of Pleasure: A Reflection on Youth and Drugs. Wellesley Hills, MA: Independent School Pr., 1983.

Richard A. Hawley
A School Answers Back: Responding to Student Drug Use. Rockville, MD: American Council for Drug Education, 1984.

Helen C. Jones and Paul W. Lovinger
The Marijuana Question. New York: Dodd, Mead & Co., 1985.

Robert E. Long, ed.
Drugs and American Society. Bronx, NY: H.W. Wilson, 1986.

Ruth Macklin
Behavior Control. Englewood Cliffs, NJ: Prentice Hall, 1981.

Peggy Mann
Twelve Is Too Old. New York: Woodmere Press, 1985.

Thomas H. Murray et al., eds.
Feeling Good and Doing Better. Clifton, NJ: The Humana Printer, 1984.

Gabriel G. Nahas
Marijuana in Science and Medicine. New York: Raven Printers, Publishers, 1984.

Paul Sanberg
Prescription Narcotics: The Addictive Painkillers. Edgemont, PA: Chelsea House Publishers, 1985.

Paul Sanberg
Over-the-Counter Drugs: Harmless or Hazardous? Edgemont, PA: Chelsea House Publishers, 1986.

Solomon Snyder
The Encyclopedia of Psychoactive Drugs: Marijuana. Edgemont, PA: Chelsea House Publishers, 1986.

Carlton E. Turner
Marijuana Controversy. Rockville, MD: American Council for Drug Education, 1981.

Gail Winger
Valium: The Tranquil Trap. Edgemont, PA: Chelsea House Publishers, 1986.

N.E. Zinberg
Drug, Set and Setting: The Basis for Controlled Intoxicant Use. New Haven, CT: Yale University Press, 1984.

Index

210

Please remember that this is a library book,
and that it belongs only temporarily to each
person who uses it. Be considerate. Do
not write in this, or any, library book.